BLIND FAITH

MY LIFE

To: Jennifer

- VOLUME I -

You are Blessed
To Be A Blessing
Your Best Day
are Right infront
of you.
Go Bravely!

JUNEGRID MARY BAKER

Jungud Bn

7/8/23

TRILOGY
CHRISTIAN
PUBLISHING

Trilogy Christian Publishers

A Wholly Owned Subsidary of Trinity Broadcasting Network

2442 Michelle Drive

Tustin, CA 92780

For information, address Trilogy Christian Publishing

Rights Department, 2442 Michelle Drive, Tustin, Ca 92780.

Trilogy Christian Publishing/TBN and colophon are trademarks of Trinity Broadcasting Network.

For information about special discounts for bulk purchases, please contact Trilogy Christian Publishing.

Manufactured in the United States of America

Trilogy Disclaimer: The views and content expressed in this book are those of the author and may not necessarily reflect the views and doctrine of Trilogy Christian Publishing or the Trinity Broadcasting Network.

10 9 8 7 6 5 4 3 2 1

Library of Congress Cataloging-in-Publication Data is available.

ISBN 979-8-88738-683-6

ISBN 979-8-88738-684-3 (ebook)

Junegrid Baker's Poem

"My Missionary Song"

Lord, I want to be a witness

To the ends of the earth;

I want the world to know

That you have saved my soul.

Lord, I'll go and let them know

Your Salvation is pure and true.

There is no one else but you,

Who can save their dying souls.

"Lord, I'll go

To the uttermost parts of the earth;

You are with me

To comfort me."

Lord, I see the boys and girls, the youth and adults, too.

Pain is in their heart,

They need a touch from you!

"Lord, I'll go

To the uttermost parts of the earth;

You are with me,

To comfort me."

Lord, since I was a little girl,

You placed a desire in my heart,

To be a missionary for you,

To preach Your Gospel True.

And now, after some twenty years,

I'm fulfilling Your Perfect Will,

As Isaiah said to you,

"Here I am! Send thou me!"

"Lord, I'll go

To the uttermost ends of the earth;

You are with me,

To comfort me."

"Go, ye therefore, and teach all nations, Go! Go! Go!

Go, ye therefore, and teach all nations, Go! Go! Go!

Baptizing them in the Name of the Father, The Son, and Holy

Ghost.

Go! Go! Go!"

"If ye love me, truly love, me, Feed my sheep!

If ye love me, truly love, me, Feed my sheep!

Lo, I'll be with you forever and forever

Until the end of the world!

Go! Go! Go!"

"Lord, I'll go to the uttermost parts of the earth

You are with me to comfort and use me!"

"A gift from God," said her mother,"

"No, no! Don't smother!"

She went here,

And over there.

At times I got the chill!

But it was only a Ministry to fulfill!

You can be short or tall,

When you're called, you're called!

Ingrid P. Jack

Junegrid Baker's Biological Big Sister

DEDICATION

This book is written in honor of my deceased husband, who transitioned to heaven on November 26, 2022. This very sad but momentous occasion occurred the day after we celebrated our 22nd marriage anniversary in his hospital room at St. Francis hospital.

One of the fifty traits, according to my husband, that attracted him to me during our six-month courtship was my anointed singing voice.

One of my husband's noble accomplishments was to assign me to a recording studio to produce an album for a song that I penned one day during my alone time with God on the mission field in Colombia.

While I was reflecting on God's missionary call upon my life, the words of the song were downloaded from the throne room of God's Kingdom to the inner chambers of my heart in May, 1998, and I sang it for my husband when we met in May, 1999.

I titled the song "My Missionary Song," and my husband was captivated by it. God impressed upon him that his

Trinidadian wife, who served for four years as a missionary in Colombia, and later came to the United States of America, was indeed a foreigner with a word for the hour. God led him to 2 Chronicles 6:32–33, 40 to endorse his sentiments:

> Moreover concerning the stranger, which is not of Thy people Israel, but is come from a far country for thy Great Name's Sake, and Thy Mighty Hand, and Thy Stretched Out Arm, if they come and pray in this house; Then hear Thou from heaven, even from Thy Dwelling Place, and do according to all that the stranger calleth to Thee for, that all people of the earth may know Thy name, and fear Thee, as doth Thy People Israel, and may know that this house which I have built is called by Thy Name...Now, my God, let, I beseech thee, Thine eyes be open, and let thine ears be attent unto the prayer that is made in this place.

These verses are included in the beginning, middle, and end of "My Missionary Song."

I dedicate this book to my four children, Theodora, Theodoxa, Theorosa, and Theojoshua Baker, whose names were all deposited into my spirit by the Holy Spirit. Their names mean God's Gift, God's Glory, God's Rose, and God's

Deliverer, respectively.

Each conception miraculously took place in a one-fallopian-tube womb between the ages of forty to forty-six years of age. That was indeed a modern-day Sarah stunt.

I reiterate the words of Joshua 24:15: "As for me and my house we will serve the Lord."

As each of my children read this book, the missionary anointing that is embedded in their lives will gush forth like rivers of living water, catapulting them to reach their generation for Jesus, propelling them to be world changers.

Acknowledgements and Thanks

I acknowledge and thank God to the utmost for giving me the boldness to be as transparent as He wants me to be as I undertake the writing of *Blind Faith:* My Life.

Junegrid Baker:

My heart is stirred by a noble theme

As I recite my verses for the King.

My tongue is the pen of a skillful writer.

God, My King:

Listen, daughter, and pay careful attention.

Forget your people and your father's house.

Let the King be enthralled by your beauty.

Honor him, for He is your Lord.

Psalm 45: 1, 10, 11

I sincerely acknowledge and thank all who responded to my request to recommend and endorse my book, *Blind Faith,* without even having read it. "You all indeed acted by "Blind Faith," and you did exceptionally well. It would seem that you did in fact preview it because of the veracity of the content that you provided. You all have demonstrated the true meaning of "being instant in season and out of season" (2 Timothy 4:2).

My acknowledgments would be incomplete if I did not pay tribute to my deceased husband by including the eulogy that I wrote for him.

TRIBUTE TO MY HUSBAND, ERNEST BAKER

EULOGY TO MY HUSBAND, ERNEST BAKER

CELEBRATING THE LIFE OF ERNEST BAKER, Jr.

January 7, 1949 – November 26, 2021

Good day to all you wonderful people,

Thank you for attending my husband's "Celebration of Life Service" today. I would like to preface my eulogy to my husband, Ernest Baker, by stating that, according to a prophetess whom God allowed to be with me at by husband's bedside, "Ernest was transitioned to heaven in a chariot of fire with angels. He was also seen in heaven with some small basketballs behind him, and he was teaching children to play basketball." My husband was passionate about basketball. In his youthful life, he was a basketball star and a coach, and the prophetess did not have a clue about that. My husband had a heart for young people and was a "father to many."

That ministry of fatherhood was reflected in his television program "Absalom, O, Absalom," which he produced and directed in Tucson for ten years. These were the words that David echoed when he heard that his son Absalom was dead: "O my son Absalom! My son, my son Absalom! If only I had died instead of you—O Absalom, my son, my son!" (2 Samuel 18:33). One of his favorite verses that supported his TV ministry was taken from Malachi 4:6: "And He will restore the hearts of the fathers to their children, and the hearts of the children to their fathers, lest I come and smite the land with a curse."

Our relationship all started with one question: "Can you kindly help transport this pot of chicken and potato soup and sandwiches to feed the poor and homeless in the nearby park?" In the month of May 1999, I was serving as the voluntary interim director at the Tucson Prayer House in Arizona, and God had spoken to me to start a ministry to the destitute in the park, just as Jesus did. I found a list of names of the board members of the Prayer House. Ernest was the first name that I called, and he readily came to help. We just knew that God had orchestrated our meeting, and we got married six months after, on Thanksgiving Day, November 25, 1999. Ernest and I celebrated twenty-two years of marriage on Thanksgiving Day, November 25, 2021, and he died the following day on November 26, 2021.

The last six months of Ernest's life were the best I had ever seen him in our twenty-two years of marriage. He became enraptured with the ministry of Pastor Sharon and Pastor Paul, and he was overwhelmingly blessed by all that he saw and experienced. For my husband to love a female pastor and submit to her was a miracle. To love and respect a pastor who was twice as young as he was and who could be his grandson was a miracle. What I am going to say now is not for any other purpose than to show you the major transformation that God made in my husband.

Before I came to Victory Church in June 2019, I was a YouTube member for six months from January to June 2019. I would sit on the love seat in my bedroom and watch Pastor Paul preach. I would invite my husband to sit alongside me to attend online church too. He would say, "Turn off that white boy; I do not want to hear that white boy." I can only tell you now that when my husband came and saw the supernatural work that God was doing here, he fell in love with that white boy, Pastor Paul, and his ministry. He fell in love with Pastor Sharon and her ministry. He fell in love with the church and the people. He was like the woman of Samaria when she had the encounter with Jesus, and she went back to her village shouting, "Come see a man who told me of all things."

Each time my husband came home from a meeting, I would overhear him on his phone talking to his siblings about what he was experiencing there and telling them to come and experience what he was experiencing. My husband was enthralled by the different ethnicities. I no longer had to wake up my husband as I had to in Arizona, He was up and ready and excited to go, and left behind those who were not ready, and said, "Every tub has to sit on its own bottom." He was unstoppable. He completed the Growth Track protocol, He filled out his Dream Team application, He was planning to get involved in altar ministry, He thought of leading a connect group, He went to men's prayer group on Saturday morning at

7:00. He would come back home and report to me that eighty men had gotten together, and they were of diverse backgrounds. They prayed together, and they called upon him to pray and to minister.

He started attending the 8:00 a.m. prayer group on Tuesday and Thursday and expressed to me the joy and liberty that he experienced in the prayer group with the women who were indeed prayer warriors. He called them the wailing and the cunning women, as stated in Jeremiah 9: 17–19. On one occasion, Ernest's younger brother was almost dying from COVID and he stood proxy for him, and the women prayed for his brother's healing. God answered the prayer, and Ernest's brother was completely healed. Ernest could not stop sharing that testimony. Ernest always longed to see signs and wonders following the Word.

He joined the men's discipleship group on a Tuesday night, and he would tell me about the anointed times he had. He was looking forward to graduate with his classmates, but my husband was such an outstanding and excellent student that he graduated before them. He graduated into heaven. God really has a sense of humor. He makes me laugh so many times just to see that His ways are unsearchable and past finding out. I was happy when I was told that Pastor Ty would be printing a certificate for him. Ernest loved Pastor Ty and spoke very highly of him and all the men on his team. He told me that his accountability prayer partner in the group was a medical doctor, and they would often call and pray for each other. The last discipleship class he attended was November 9, and that night he reported to me how supernatural the class was by saying, "I cannot take it. It is beyond me—it is so anointed!"

Prior to that week, my husband decided to go on a fast and that very day, I heard my husband singing out very loudly in the bedroom, praying vociferously and profusely in tongues. I was in the living room teaching my Zoom classes and I literally felt the tremors and vibrations of his praise filling the house. I had never heard him burst out into praise in such a vocal manner; I was so proud of my husband. I did not want him to stop. I wanted him to continue experiencing that deep intimacy with the Holy Spirit. My husband wanted to ensure that all of his family members were sold out to Jesus. I overheard him telling each family member and friend that he communicated with that he was going to sell out to Jesus—that he was going all the way with Him!

In closing, family members and friends, Ernest is very happy in heaven. He was ready to go. He did not want to be hooked up to any machine. He did not want the BiPAP and ventilator. He blatantly refused it. He just wanted to die a natural death. On Wednesday he was about to have a cardiac arrest and the doctor told me to ask him if he would try the intubator. Even though he was lethargic, he acquiesced. His life was prolonged to give family and friends the opportunity to express final remarks of love and encouragement to him, pray with him, and sing for him. My husband could hear his children, friends, and relatives, but he could not respond to them. His organs were shutting down, and by Friday he was in a very critical condition. The doctors indicated to me that the machines were loud and very distracting to my husband. The machines were gradually unplugged so as to allow my husband his wish to go home peacefully without any encumbrances of machines. A chariot of fire with angels was awaiting him and he went up to meet His Lord and Savior Jesus Christ.

Ernest is among that cloud of witnesses that is spoken of in Hebrews 12:1. He is looking down right now, and he is seeing this "Celebration of His Life." Ernest's desire for each of his family members and friends is for them to follow in his footsteps. Take up the baton and run the race with the same fervor and excitement that he exhibited in these last six months. Do not compromise! Be totally sold out to Jesus. Do not be lukewarm. Be on fire for Jesus. Ernest has "fought the good fight, [he] has finished the course, [he] has kept the faith, henceforth there is laid up for [him] a crown of righteousness, which the Lord, the righteous judge shall give [him] at that day, and not to [him] only, but unto all of them also that love is appearing" (2 Timothy 4:7–8).

I love you honey,

Junegrid Baker

11/30/2021

CONTENTS

FOREWORD

My name is Godfrey Lord, a minister of the Gospel of Jesus Christ. I have been a pastor, evangelist, and a behavioral counselor for many years, and I am still doing so.

I am honored to be chosen to write the foreword for this book "Blind Faith." I met Junegrid Baker in Tucson, Arizona about twenty-six years ago. Mrs. Baker is a native of Trinidad and Tobago. She is a young lady with high expectations, and she departed from her family to do God's calling for her life.

Let me now say that stepping out of your comfort zone is not easy. One must be willing to explore the unknown with a blind faith perspective. For instance, you might have once had a dream, as did Junegrid in her early childhood, believing that someday she would acquaint herself with Oral Roberts University. Notwithstanding, her dream was deluded because of her trials of life, both academically and in her personal lifestyle.

I am acquainted with her family and many of her scholars, both locally and abroad. She is one who demonstrates high excellence in whatever she pursues, and now, as an accomplished author of life experience with herself and family, impacting others to develop a life-changing miraculous encounter in life.

The information that you will glean by reading this book will motivate you beyond your expectations. How does anyone depart from their comfort zone to an unknown location without blind faith? Allow me to call your attention to Noah in the Bible, whom the Creator God told to build Him a boat because it was going to rain. Noah, not having a knowledge of what rain was, operated by blind faith, obeyed God and the boat was completed by the help of God and his faith to believe. Now let me call your attention to a man by the name of Abraham. God spoke to him to leave his family and go to a far country, a land he had never seen before. Stepping out by blind faith, he left his parents and departed as God told him.

Likewise, the above information you have read is a tangible life experience found in the life of Mrs. Baker. Junegrid Baker departed from her country to minister God's Word to a place and country she had never been before. Similarly, she departed from Yuma, Arizona to Tulsa, Oklahoma with blind faith to further her education in the state of her childhood dream, to attend Oral Roberts University, where she is pursuing a doctoral degree in ministry.

One can learn through blind faith to depart, not knowing

the outcome or what to expect. When you have chosen to make such moves, by faith, you believe that all will be good in the end. The term "better the end of a matter than the beginning" is all by faith. Having had the experience of reading this book will motivate you to step out with blind faith to pursue your dream. Mrs. Baker encountered her blind faith to mobilize herself; however, it did not come without much testing and trials. However, she is staying in the course to the finishing life. I must say that I have had many such experiences of blind faith in my life. The victory is to endure to the end. It is not easy to step out on blind faith. This book will motivate you and others as it has impacted me to know the author and the life-changing experience one can glean from reading this book.

REVEREND GODFREY LORD

PREFACE

Blind Faith is very aptly defined in Hebrews 11:1 (NKJV): "Now faith is the substance of things hoped for, the evidence of things not seen."

- Blind faith is essentially acting in obedience without fully understanding, seeing, and knowing all the answers.

- Blind faith is knowing, believing, and accepting what God prompts or instructs us to do, without doubting, disbelieving, or questioning, even when from a human point of view His directives seem unclear, unreasonable, and impossible.

- Blind faith represents the blinders that horses wear. These blinkers cover the rear and side vision of the horse and prevent him from seeing behind and beside him. The horse is forced to focus only on a forward direction so that they will not panic or be distracted by what they see around them.

- Blind faith causes us to keep our faces like flint and march forward, paying attention to the race by doing what God tells us to do without any distractions.

- Blind faith is not blind, because as the graphic on the cover of my book displays, we are being led by the One who sees and knows all things, the One who knows the end from the beginning, the One who sees the big picture, and the One who knows how the story will end.
- Blind faith, simply put, is trusting God's leading.

This book is primarily a compilation of anecdotes of my life experiences when blind faith was demonstrated.

The writing of this book is, in fact, an act of blind faith because it is devoid of order and organizational skills. It is filled with spontaneity and on-the-spur-of-the-moment recollections of events that reflect blind faith.

I was motivated to write this book on May 22, 2022, after Rena heard my 2022 graduation speech for the very first Oral Roberts University (ORU) Veterans Graduation service. Rena immediately and authoritatively retorted, "You've got to write a book!" She fearlessly proceeded to submit to me *Blind Faith* as the title of the book.

For you to understand why Rena responded in such a vehement and timely manner, it behooves me to allow you, my audience, to become privy to the contents of my speech in the very first chapter of my book—Chapter One: Junegrid Baker's Graduation Speech for ORU's Veterans and Dependents Award Ceremony 4/30/2022.

Readers, I must let you know that I just recalled that prior to meeting Rena, the suggestion to write a book came from four of my intercessory prayer partners who attended my graduation ceremony for ORU's veterans and dependents on April 30, 2022. After hearing my valedictorian speech, Janet complimented me, beamed with a broad smile, stared into my eyes, and said, "You are such a detailed, transparent writer and an eloquent speaker! You need to write a book! Her husband, Galen smiled and nodded in agreement. Deborah and Maria fixed their eyes on me, and they both said that my speech was very emotional and touching. They both concurred that I should write a book.

Chapter One

Junegrid Baker's Graduation Speech for ORU's Veterans and Dependents Award Ceremony

4/30/2022

"Good day President Wilson, Mr. William Beck, administrators, professors, faculty, staff, family, friends, and fellow graduates—veterans and dependents.

I deem it a great honor and privilege to be the graduation speaker for ORU's first ever Veterans and Dependents Award Ceremony. I have been asked to share about my ORU journey and address the graduating class of 2022.

My ORU journey started at age eleven, in 1973, soon after I decided to accept Jesus as Lord and Savior of my life.

Does anyone recognize this book? It will probably date me. This book, *A Daily Guide to Miracles*, by Oral Roberts, marks the beginning of my ORU trajectory.

I don't quite remember how this book came into my possession in Trinidad, my country of origin, but at that young age, I started reading it and using it as my daily devotional guide.

As the years transpired, I became oblivious to this book, and the memory of it was reignited in November 2018 when I brought my daughter to the ORU Quest Scholarship weekend.

This journey to ORU was an eighteen-hour nonstop drive from Arizona to Oklahoma, just to get my daughter there on time. Our late departure from Arizona resulted because, at the last minute, my husband changed his mind about all six of us going as a family to support our daughter.

Guess what? Yours truly had to take up the slack to ensure that our daughter got to her ORU orientation on time. There were three occasions when I fell asleep while driving, but God miraculously protected us.

Backtracking a little, my daughter was at the point of graduating from her high school senior year and was trying to decide what college to attend. As I was watching TBN (Trinity Broadcasting Network), Robert Morris came on and announced that his daughter attended ORU, and he spoke highly of her amazing experiences there.

I quickly called my daughter and recommended ORU for her to attend. She immediately expressed disinterest and rushed back into her room. She returned to me fifteen minutes after, very excitedly, stating that she went to the ORU website, liked what she saw, and enthusiastically proceeded to fill out the freshman application form.

God had great secret plans for my life as I sacrificially and lovingly accompanied my daughter to ORU. Arriving at ORU, when I saw the immense diversity of the ORU population and the Christian love exhibited both by students and administration, the only way I could describe ORU was "Heaven on Earth!"

As if that was not enough, when I went to the ORU Prayer Tower, God spoke to me about my entire family relocating from Arizona to Oklahoma.

God started putting everything into place because when God gives a vision, He always makes the provision. As we got back to Arizona, God started providing a house for us in Tulsa. God opened the doors for my children to be enrolled at Victory Christian School in Tulsa. I was promised a Spanish teaching job at a certain school in Tulsa, and I was already an online member of Victory Christian Church in Tulsa while in Arizona.

Being a Christian is not always a bed of roses! To get from the vision to the provision is not a smooth road. There are many hurdles and detours along the way. I wish I could stand up here and tell you that everything aligned easily and peacefully—that I got from point A to point B unchallenged. It was not so at all.

My entire family was opposed to the move from Arizona to Oklahoma. Even after God gave all six of us an angelic visitation to confirm the move, doubts prevailed. As nine of us, including three cousins from New York, were having dinner at Texas Roadhouse to celebrate our daughter's senior high school graduation, a "giant-sized" Caucasian gentleman appeared at the table where my husband and I were sitting opposite to each other. He shook my hand and said in a very loud tone of voice, "So, you're going to Oklahoma!"

That was the last topic that I wanted to broach, given the negative disposition of my family towards the transition. However, I mustered up some boldness and said with unashamed confidence, "Yes! I am!" When I looked beside me for the gentleman, he was not there. I turned to my husband and asked him if he saw where the gentleman went, and he said, "No." I promptly and boldly said to my husband, "We just had an angelic visitation!"

Unfortunately, my family continued to resist the God-ordained relocation from Arizona to Oklahoma even though God sent an angel to confirm it! In June 2019, as I was driving into Oklahoma with my twelve-year-old son, God impressed upon me that Oklahoma would no longer be known as a state of tornadoes, but as a state of revival. Well, I was excited to be part of that Revival! However, when I got to Tulsa, I faced a major disappointment when I was told that the promised job of a Spanish teacher was given to someone else.

The devil came whispering in my ear, "Did you really hear from God to resign from your teaching job in Arizona to come here? How are you going to live? Is this the beginning of the revival that you said you heard of from God?"

Some weeks after, an opportunity opened for me to be a success coach. However, even though my interview was successful, and I was given an orientation for the job position, I waited for weeks but was never called to start the job. A family member later told me that a request was made for me to be preempted from the job because the person felt uncomfortable being at the same university with me. I remembered what Paul said in Romans 7:21: "When we strive to do good, evil is present." I quickly edified myself and waged war against evil, declaring, "I am more than a conqueror in Jesus."

It was so easy for me to become bitter, hateful, and resentful, but I chose not to. I could have said, like the children of Israel, "God, why did you bring me to Tulsa to kill me? Why did you bring me here to die?" I could have decided to return to Arizona to try to recuperate my previous teaching job! But I held on to the vision God gave me and chose to forgive, believing that all things work together for good to those who love the Lord and are called together for His purposes. God answered my prayers over and beyond.

It is exactly what Paul says in Colossians 3:20: "God is able to do exceedingly abundantly above all that we ask or think, according to the power that works in us."

When I relocated to Tulsa, it was not my original plan to become a student at ORU. However, God had ulterior motives for my life. I was approved to enroll in the Masters of Christian Ministry in the spring of 2020, then upon Dr. Loescher's recommendation, I switched to Master of Divinity in the fall of that same year, 2020.

Additionally, my field study at ORU opened the doors for me to do my internship at the Iglesia Hispana Victory Church, and at the end of my internship, I was asked to stay on to teach at their Bible Institute.

I am presently pursuing my Doctorate in Ministry. How great is our God! His ways and plans are past finding out. They are unsearchable!

Even though my husband constantly said to me, "Forever studying and never coming to an understanding," it was very interesting and ironic that when he eventually submitted entirely to God's will and relocated fully to Tulsa, that he began engaging in some deep studies too in the Men's Discipleship class at Victory Christian Church. Did I tell him, "Forever studying and never coming to an understanding?" By no means! I was happy that he was studying! My steadfastness and commitment to the call of God on my life to study to show myself approved unto God, a workman who needs not to be ashamed, rightly dividing the Word of truth, motivated my husband to do likewise.

Thank God I did not let my husband's words discourage and deter me! Critics usually get converted!

The last six months of my husband's life were the best I had ever seen him in our twenty-two years of marriage. He was on fire for Jesus and was at a spiritual height that was uncontrollable.

It has been five months now since he transitioned to heaven, and even though he is not here today physically to witness

my graduation, he is with the great cloud of witnesses men-
tioned in Hebrews 12:1, looking down and cheering me on.

Graduates, "Let's not cast away our confidence, which has
great reward, for we have need of endurance, so that after we
have done the will of God, we receive the promise" (Hebrews
10:35, 36). I want to encourage us to fight the good fight of
faith. Let us finish the race. Let us keep the faith. For there is a
crown of Righteousness laid up for us, and the Lord, the Righteous Judge will give it to us on that Day" (2 Timothy 4: 7–8).

Let us keep our face as flint and do what God has called us
to do.

Let us run with the vision that God has given to us.

Let us not tarry!

Let us not retreat!

"Write the vision and make it plain on tablets that he may
run who reads it. For the vision is yet for an appointed time:
but at the end it will speak, and it will not lie. Though it tar-
ries, wait for it. Because it will surely come, it will not tarry!"
(Habakkuk 2:2–3).

God is not finished with us yet! Our best days are right in
front of us! Our eyes have not seen, our ears have not heard,
neither has it entered into our hearts the things that God has

prepared for us because we love Him.

Graduates, as Oral Roberts, the founder of this University charged us,

"Let's go change the world.

"Let's go where God's voice is heard small.

"Let's go where God's healing power is not known.

"Let's go even to the uttermost bounds of the earth."

Graduates, "Let's go change the world!"

"HE GIVES HIS ANGELS CHARGE OVER ME TO KEEP ME IN ALL OF MY WAYS."

(PSALM 91:11)

"THE LORD IS MY LIGHT AND MY SALVATION; WHOM SHALL I FEAR?"

(PSALM 27:1)

CHAPTER TWO

JUNEGRID'S PRAYER

"A GIFT FROM GOD," SAID HER MOTHER,"

"NO, NO! DON'T SMOTHER!"

SHE WENT HERE,

AND OVER THERE.

AT TIMES I GOT THE CHILL!

BUT IT WAS ONLY A MINISTRY TO FULFILL!

YOU CAN BE SHORT OR TALL,

WHEN YOU'RE CALLED, YOU'RE CALLED!

INGRID P. JACK

JUNEGRID BAKER'S BIOLOGICAL BIG SISTER

***

I HAVE KNOWN JUNEGRID BAKER FOR MORE THAN FORTY YEARS. WE WERE TEENAGERS TOGETHER AT THE ST. AUGUSTINE EVANGELICAL BIBLE CHURCH IN TRINIDAD AND WERE CLOSE FRIENDS WHEN WE ATTENDED UNIVERSITY TOGETHER ON THE SAME FACULTY.

JUNE, AS I CALL HER, IS A LOVER OF GOD, OF HIS WORD, AND OF HIS WAYS, ALWAYS WILLING TO FOLLOW WHERE SHE BELIEVES HE IS LEADING HER. SHE LAUNCHES OUT IN FAITH AND TRUSTS GOD TO TAKE CARE OF THE DETAILS. IT WAS BLIND FAITH

THAT PROPELLED HER TO LEAVE A SECURE TEACHING JOB IN TRINIDAD AND PROCEED TO COLOMBIA, SOUTH AMERICA AS A MISSIONARY, NOT KNOWING WHERE SHE WAS GOING TO LIVE OR HOW SHE WAS GOING TO SURVIVE. ALL SHE KNEW WAS THAT GOD HAD COMMISSIONED HER TO GO. YEARS LATER IN THE USA SHE TOOK A LEAP OF FAITH AGAIN WHEN, SIMPLY OUT OF OBEDIENCE TO GOD, SHE MOVED FROM ARIZONA TO TULSA WITH HER SON, NOT KNOWING WHAT AWAITED HER THERE, BUT CONFIDENT THAT THE GOD WHO CALLED HER THERE WOULD TAKE CARE OF THEM THERE. THE INSTANCES WHERE SHE PRACTICED BLIND FAITH, AND THE RESULTANT BLESSINGS, ARE A TESTIMONY TO WHAT GOD CAN DO IN A LIFE THAT IS SIMPLY WILLING TO TRUST HIM AND DO AS HE DIRECTS.

WENDY BASCOMBE-EDWARDS, B.A; DIPED

***

My dear readers, there is no doubt in my mind that after reading my graduation speech, you are echoing what Rena confirmed to me: "Write a book!"

Yes. You are right. I am writing this book because I have something to say. I have a profound message to transmit to you:

"Walk by faith and not by sight" (2 Corinthians 5:7).

"Now faith is the substance of things hoped for, the evidence of things not seen" (Hebrews 11:1).

The theme "faith" is all wrapped up in my book *Blind Faith.*

"Without faith it is impossible to please God. He who comes to God must believe that He is a rewarder of those who diligently seek Him" (Hebrews 11:6).

"The just shall live by faith" (Hebrews 10:38; Romans 1:17; Galatians 3:11).

My prayer for you, my precious audience, is that as you continue to read this book, you will appreciate the importance of living a faith-filled life instead of a fear-filled one. I pray that you will be obedient to God and say "Yes" to Him in all that he tells you to do and speak. Utter Isaiah's words to God's question, "Whom shall I send?" "Here am I, send me!" (Isaiah 6:8) Obey the words of Mary, Jesus' mother, "Whatsoever He says to you, do it!" (John 2:5). As you step out, operate in blind faith, and trust in Him, God will step in, give you sight, and lead you all the way. "For I know the plans I have for you, plans to prosper you, and not to harm you, plans to give you hope and a future" (Jeremiah 29:11).

"HE MAKES WAYS IN THE WILDERNESS AND RIVERS

IN THE DESERT

GOD HAS ENGRAVED ME ON THE PALM OF HIS

HANDS."

(ISAIAH 49:16)

CHAPTER THREE

RENA—A PROPHET'S REWARD

"THERE ARE PEOPLE WHO TALK ABOUT FAITH AND THERE ARE PEOPLE WHO WALK IN FAITH" (JAMES 2:18). JUNEGRID BAKER WALKED THE TALK BY STEPPING UP AND STEPPING OUT TO ANSWER GOD'S CALL. AND SHE FOUND GOD TO BE WHO HE SAID HE IS: FAITHFUL AND TRUE. MAY HER STORY BE AN INSPIRATION AND AN ENCOURAGEMENT TO US ALL.

DANFORD MAPP, BSc., MSc., PMP

GRADUATE OF LANGHAM PREACHING INSTITUTE

WORSHIP LEADER CHAGUANAS EVANGELICAL BIBLE CHURCH

THIS BOOK, WITHOUT DOUBT, IS ONE OF THE MOST IMPACTING AND MOVING TESTIMONIES OF SUCCESS-FUL NAVIGATION THROUGH LIFE'S JOURNEY THAT YOU WILL EVER READ. JUNEGRID BAKER HAS TOLD THE TRUTH AND NOTHING BUT THE TRUTH IN THIS EPIC ACCOUNT OF HER LIFE. HERS IS A DEPICTION OF AMAZING GRIT AND DETERMINATION, LIKE JOHNA-THAN AND HIS ARMOR BEARER CLIMBING UP THE STEEP AND DANGEROUS RIDGE IN PURSUIT OF VIC-TORY OVER THE MASSIVE GARRISONS OF THE PHILIS-TINES, PERCHED TO ATTACK ISRAEL FROM THE HILL,

AS FOUND IN 1 SAMUEL 13-14. SHE NEVER LOOKED BACK ONCE GOD CLEARED THE PATH BEFORE HER, AND SHE BEGAN TO MARCH FORWARD; THIS IS THE GLORIOUS RESULT—A SUCCESS STORY INDEED. CONGRATULATIONS TO JUNE, HER HUSBAND AND FAMILY. EVERY YOUNG, UNMARRIED, OR TROUBLED WOMAN SHOULD READ THIS INSPIRING BOOK.

PASTOR AND APOSTLE DR. VERNON JOSEPH DUNCAN

***

By now, you must be wondering who Rena is. Rena came on the scene because I operated in blind faith. My immediate response to Rena when she called and told me of her uncomfortable living arrangement was, "You were on my mind. I was about to call you. My house is God's house. You are welcome to come and stay here. Please pray about it."

Rena had been living in Tulsa for three months and had recently started attending the daily 6:30 a.m. Intercessory Prayer Group at Victory Christian Church. One morning, after I prayed, I excused myself early, stating that I needed to take an Uber to go to Enterprise Car Rental to pick up a car because my mechanic was doing some work on my car. Rena was one of two people to retort promptly, "Oh no! You are not catching an Uber. I'll take you." Even though I tried to refuse the offer,

I humbly and gratefully accepted. Throughout the ten-minute trip to Enterprise, Rena and I engaged in continual conversation, elevating Jesus and testifying about the goodness of God.

Our encounter was a divine setup and God was preparing me to take a leap of faith two weeks after to invite Rena into my home. It appeared that time had stopped during Rena's first night in my home. The whole scenario reminded me of perhaps what took place in the Upper Room where the disciples were told by Jesus to wait in prayer and fasting for the Promise of the Father. We were basking and lingering in God's presence. Rena and I sat in the living room for possibly three consecutive hours thanking and praising Jesus. We prayed in the Spirit and with understanding. We shared about the love of Jesus, and personal faith experiences.

As we proceeded in spontaneous dialogue, we both sensed that indeed God had orchestrated our meeting. That divine encounter was for God's glory. It was also for us to speak into each other's lives and edify each other. "As iron sharpens iron, so one person sharpens another" (Proverbs 27:17).

Even as I am reviewing this chapter, I must let you know, dear readers that the divine encounter between Rena and myself was ordained by God for five intensive weeks of mutual Spirit-filled ministry, and then it was time to move on to the next page of our individual lives. That is what blind faith does—it causes doors to open, and it causes doors to close. It is important for us to know and catch the right season as penned in the beautiful poetry in Ecclesiastes 3: 1-8:

> To everything *there is* a season,
>
> A time for every purpose under heaven:
>
> A time to be born,
>
> And a time to die;
>
> A time to plant,
>
> And a time to pluck *what is* planted;
>
> A time to kill,
>
> And a time to heal;
>
> A time to break down,
>
> And a time to build up;
>
> A time to weep,
>
> And a time to laugh;
>
> A time to mourn,
>
> And a time to dance;
>
> A time to cast away stones,
>
> And a time to gather stones;

A time to embrace,

And a time to refrain from embracing;

A time to gain,

And a time to lose;

A time to keep,

And a time to throw away;

A time to tear,

And a time to sew;

A time to keep silence,

And a time to speak;

A time to love,

And a time to hate;

A time of war,

And a time of peace.

"FEAR NOT, FOR I AM WITH YOU; BE NOT DISMAYED,

FOR I AM YOUR GOD; I WILL STRENGTHEN YOU,

I WILL HELP YOU, I WILL UPHOLD YOU WITH MY

RIGHTEOUS RIGHT HAND."

(ISAIAH 41:10)

"GOD, KEEP ME AS THE APPLE OF YOUR EYE."

(PSALM 17:8)

Chapter Four

My Personal Testimony and Experiences

I MET JUNEGRID WHEN WE WERE BOTH IN OUR TEENS AND HAVE SEEN AND ADMIRED HER UNRELENTING FAITH IN HER GOD GROW FROM STRENGTH TO UN-QUESTIONABLE RELIANCE ON GOD. SOMETIMES SHE HAD TO WALK ALONE BECAUSE OF HER OBEDIENCE TO GOD, FOR WHICH SHE WAS REWARDED. I BELIEVE YOU, READERS OF THIS TESTIMONY, WILL CERTAINLY BE INSPIRED TO MOVE FORWARD IN YOUR WALK WITH GOD.

GLORIA WARD

RETIRED TEACHER

BLIND FAITH IS A "MUST READ" IF YOU WANT YOUR FAITH IN GOD TO GROW. FOLLOW ABRAHAM'S AND JUNEGRID'S EXAMPLES. WHEN GOD SPEAKS, OBEY IMMEDIATELY. DON'T ALLOW YOUR MIND TO ASK FOR DETAILS AND UNDERSTANDING. IF IT IS A GOD-DREAM, IT IS FAR PAST ANY HUMAN ABILITY TO COMPREHEND. BE LIKE REINHARD BONNKE WHEN HE RECEIVED A WORD FROM THE LORD, "I FEEL THAT THE EYES OF GOD ARE ON ME, AND I WANT HIM TO SEE THAT WHEN

HE SPEAKS, I JUMP." MAY EACH READER OF THIS BOOK
PREPARE THEMSELVES TO JUMP IMMEDIATELY WHEN
THEY HEAR THE VOICE OF GOD AND SAY, "YES, SIR!"
IN THE POWERFUL NAME OF JESUS, ENJOY JUNEGRID'S
ADVENTURES IN *BLIND FAITH*. SHALOM.

DEBORAH ANDREWS

B.S. ELEMENTARY EDUCATION;

M.S IN SCHOOL GUIDANCE AND COUNSELING

(RETIRED TWENTY-SEVEN YEARS)

***

During the course of the writing of this book, the Holy
Spirit is prompting me to share my personal testimony with
you. As you read it, you will encounter many incidents where I
operated in blind faith. "My heart is stirred by a noble theme as
I recite my verses for the king; my pen is the pen of a skillful
writer" (Psalm 45:1).

My major ministry experiences started when God called
me at thirty-three-and-a-half years of age to be a missionary in
Colombia, South America, in 1995. I spent three months in sol-
itude with God from October to December 1994 to seek Him
for more direction.

I then resigned from my teaching career in Trinidad, moved out by faith, like Abraham did, not knowing exactly where I was going, but simply knowing that God had called me to go to Colombia, and I had to obey.

Upon my arrival in Colombia, I thought that I would have to take a taxi from San Cristobal in Venezuela to cross the border and go to Cúcuta, Colombia. However, as I alighted from the plane, there was an unknown pastor, along with two assistants, holding a placard with my name inscribed in big, bold letters. What a miracle! How great is our God! When God gives the vision, He has already made the provision!

Pastor Nelson took me to his home, where his wife had prepared a sumptuous dinner for me. As I took a quick glimpse at the dinner table, I observed some 'foreign food." I immediately remembered that God had warned me during my preparation time in seclusion with Him in Trinidad that I should not go to Colombia and long for my Trinidadian food. I intentionally smiled and expressed overt gratitude for the lavish dinner, but silently said a prayer, "Dear God, please help my stomach!" I very happily survived the meal, which I discovered was called *caldo*. It consisted of potatoes and half-cooked eggs, and it turned out to be my favorite Colombian dish. When I returned to Trinidad some years later, I prepared caldo for my mother and she loved it.

After dinner, as I entered the living room of Pastor Nelson's house, a young teenager approached me with a huge kitchen knife and said, "I'm going to kill you! I knew a black lady was coming here, and I was waiting for you!" I was not certain that I was prepared for such an initiation, but Pastor Nelson quickly smiled and told me very authoritatively, "It's okay, June. Just put your hand on her head and rebuke satan from her in the name of Jesus!" I did exactly as Pastor Nelson told me, and the teenage girl instantaneously began to vomit blood. That marked her deliverance from satanic interference and dominance in her life. Pastor Nelson later told me that she was married to satan. She had made a pact with satan which was broken that very night during the deliverance that God used me to minister to her.

Upon my arrival in Cúcuta, Colombia, the city was literally shaking from earthquakes. I was very impressed by the clitter-clatter of shoes coming into the church on the very first morning as I was praying in the annexed church at 5:00 a.m. When I turned around from where I was sitting upfront, the church was packed with students and adults who had come in to pray before they left for school and their various workplaces. How touched I was! There was a cause to pray! Earthquakes were pervading Cúcuta. Witchcraft and demonic activity were prevalent. Poverty was rampant. Prayer and fasting were the only solution to these problematic events. I remembered Jesus' words to his disciples: "Some things come only by prayer and fasting" (Matthew 17:21; Mark 9:29).

I served in the ministry of prayer and intercession, the deliverance ministry, and preaching for about one month in that Four-Square Gospel Church in Cúcuta, Colombia. I then moved on to a Four-Square Gospel Church in Bucaramanga, Colombia, where I wrote a booklet on the Holy Spirit (*El Espíritu Santo*). I sometimes served as an interpreter for Andes, another missionary who had relocated to Colombia from Trinidad about two years before I did. I helped him oversee a group of Colombian Bible Institute students, and I traveled to different villages to preach.

Boyacá was one of the villages where I was assigned to preach, and as I was making preparations to go there to minister, I received a message that a pastor was just shot and killed there. The host pastor asked me if I still wanted to come, and my answer was in the affirmative. God moved mightily in the church in Boyacá in the ministry of reconciliation and deliverance, and many lives were blessed.

Looking back on those four years of missionary work in Colombia, I do not seem to remember many things in the physical. I just felt that I was operating so much in the Spirit and was propelled by the Spirit that I cannot give a detailed explanation to many events in the physical realm.

After spending about two years in Bucaramanga, I moved to Bogotá, Colombia, where Pastor Gustavo of Oasis Praise Center (El Centro De la Alabanza Oasis), appointed me to be the director of the church's Bible seminary. I led in early morning intercessory prayer at the seminary from five o'clock until six o'clock, and was involved in marriage counseling, praise and worship, teaching, preaching, and deliverance at the church. During that time, I also served as an interpreter, and went to different cities like Calí, Medellín, Barranca and Barranquilla to assist the pastor in ministry.

My mother prayed that her baby would be a useful Christian boy or girl while I was in her womb. Just as my mother's words were clear and precise, God's answer to her prayer was clear and precise. God used my mother's utterance to cause His divine hands to be released upon my life, directing me into the ministry that He had for me.

Even though I grew up in a humble environment, my mother demonstrated the best love and sacrificial care that I could have ever known. She taught me how to read and write, and most of all, she read to me from the Bible. She told me Bible stories, prayed for, and with me, and taught me how to pray. She taught me the Lord's Prayer in Matthew 6:9–13, Psalm 23, and Psalm 1. God was always at the center of her life. I learned from her that JESUS is always the way to supersede poverty and lack. I do not have to succumb to inadequacies and limitations, but I can be strong with God's help and persevere to greatness.

Without this Biblical and educational foundation, I would not be where I am today. I grew up in a traditional Anglican home where my mother read the Bible to me and took me to the Anglican Church. My grandmother, who was Catholic, sometimes took me to the Catholic Church. I became a Sunday school teacher for preschoolers in the Anglican Church at the age of ten, but I became very disenchanted with the Anglican Church when I discovered the priest and his wife smoking a pipe in their parishioner's house. Being exposed to the Anglican and Catholic doctrines enabled me to see firsthand their erroneous teachings and direct myself and others away from anti-Biblical and manmade teachings.

At age eleven, I accepted Jesus as Lord and Savior of my life in a Missionary Baptist Church that was constructed obliquely opposite to my house in Curepe. I had left the Anglican Church and started attending the Missionary Baptist Church, where I got saved under the "fire and brimstone preaching" of Pastor Nimblett. He preached from Matthew 25: 1–13 about the five wise and the five foolish virgins. Fear was instilled into me because I did not want to be left behind like the five foolish virgins who missed the bridegroom because they fell asleep and were unprepared to meet him with their lamps "trimmed with oil."

Pastor Nimblett's sermon was very convincing. I was convicted, and I decided to respond to the altar call that was given at the end. I said the prayer of repentance and asked Jesus to come into my heart and be Lord and Savior of my life. I got saved out of fear of going to hell!

I was sitting next to my grandmother in the church on that Old Year's Night in 1972, and as I stood up to move forward to the altar, I literally felt something trying to pull me back. That was satan himself. Thank God I was able to overcome that demonic assault and advance towards the altar. That was the Holy Spirit!

Just as midnight struck on December 31, 1972, I surrendered my life to Jesus, and the rest is history. I must interject here that not too long after my conversion, God impressed upon me that I was going to be a missionary.

I continued going faithfully to the Missionary Baptist Church with my sister, and my Hindu and Muslim neighbors and friends who were miraculously converted to Christianity. All of my former Hindu and Muslim friends in the neighborhood were getting water baptized, but my mother, out of ignorance, forbade me from doing so under the premise that "You were born an Anglican, you will die as an Anglican. When you turn twenty-one (the age of accountability), you could do what you want!" My heart was deeply saddened at each baptism service, as the congregation sang the baptism hymn, "Shall we gather at the river where bright angels' feet have trod?" I saw my neighborhood friends being submerged in the water by the Pastor, an event that I deeply yearned for, and I even thought that I would go to hell if the second coming of Jesus were to take place before I got water baptized. I expressed my concern to some of my "baptized" friends who did their best to console me by saying that the thief on the cross who repented did not have time to be baptized, yet Jesus told him, "Today, you will be with me in Paradise" (Luke 23:43).

Unfortunately, the Missionary Baptist Church did not emphasize the full workings of the Holy Spirit, and I was not taught that it was the Holy Spirit who would endow me with the power to live the Christian life. I was struggling to live the Christian life because it was not explained to me that I had to depend on the Holy Spirit, and not on myself to live a Christian life. At age twelve, I started attending the Inter School Christian Fellowship camps during the summer, and the camp counselors clarified to me that it was the Holy Spirit who would help me to live the Christian life and capacitate me to be an obedient child to my parents. "It is the Holy Spirit who works in me both to will and to do of His good pleasure" (Philippians 2:13).

At age fourteen, I left the Missionary Baptist Church and started attending the Evangelical Christian Bible Church, where the importance of the Holy Spirit was being taught. Many of my summer camp friends were attending that church where there was a vibrant youth meeting and I wanted to be part of it.

At age fifteen, I got baptized. It was because of my persistent and heartfelt prayer that God worked a miracle and softened my mother's resilient heart. My mother attended my water baptism at the Victory Heights Bible Camp swimming pool and witnessed my open profession of my faith to the hymn "Spirit of God Descend Upon My Heart." She also accepted Jesus as Lord and Savior of her life not too long after, left the Anglican Church and started going to a Pentecostal church where she got baptized. "The effectual fervent prayer of a righteous person avails much" (James 5:14). This is one of the verses that helped me to surmount many challenging situations in my life and launched me into ministry.

At age eighteen, I started going to the University of the West Indies to study Languages and Literature, and I became involved in the InterVarsity Christian Fellowship where I learned more on the infilling and Baptism of the Holy Spirit with the evidence of speaking with tongues. I became hungry for that because speaking in tongues was not encouraged at the Evangelical church.

At age twenty-one, I obtained my Bachelor of Arts degree in Languages and Literature from the University of the West Indies, St. Augustine. On July 12, 1982, soon after submitting my thesis paper at the university, I was accosted by John, a young man who was a camper from the Inter School Christian Fellowship camps. We started dating and I believed that God confirmed him to be my marriage life partner. He attended La Romain Pentecostal Church, and occasionally I would go there too, because I hungered even more for the Baptism of the Holy Spirit with the evidence of speaking in other tongues. I continued attending St. Augustine Evangelical Church. I became a French teacher at St. Joseph's Convent, Port-of-Spain at age twenty-one in September 1982, and got engaged that same year.

Obtaining my degree in languages was used by God to prepare me for the mission field in Colombia, where I could minister effectively in the Spanish language. God was also preparing me to seek after Him continually for more, and never to become complacent or nonchalant in ministry.

At age twenty-two, I got married to that young man, and within a year, I resigned from teaching and attended the West Indies School of Theology with my husband, because I felt that God was calling me to be a missionary and not a Spanish teacher.

At age twenty-three, I started attending three different Pentecostal churches—Faith Revival Ministries, Mount Hope Pentecostal, and La Romain Pentecostal. I eventually received the Baptism of the Holy Spirit with the evidence of speaking in other tongues. After one semester at the West Indies School of Theology, I reverted to being a Spanish teacher because of financial hardships. I initiated prayer and Bible study groups at each school where I taught—Malick Senior Comprehensive, Pleasantville Senior Comprehensive, Siparia Junior Secondary, Princes Town Senior Comprehensive, Toco Composite, and Belmont Junior Secondary.

At age twenty-five, I started pastoring with my husband in Toco, a remote country area, and at age twenty-six, after one year of ministry struggle, I reintegrated into a Pentecostal church with my husband, under the pastorate of Kenneth and Kerlina Niles.

At age twenty-nine, I divorced my husband, who was continuously being unfaithful and truly unrepentant. Even though my husband was a Christian and a summer camper with the Inter School Christian Fellowship, when we met on that fateful day, he was in a backslidden stage. He told me that he had just smoked a cigarette and drunk beer, and he vowed privately to

God that he would stop because he did not want to lose me. He was also sexually promiscuous and vowed to quit. I was devastated when I learned of my husband's continuous unfaithfulness and infidelity while pastoring and preaching. I thought I had married him for a lifetime, but I had to end the marriage in divorce.

At age thirty, I started attending Divine Encounter Fellowship, became a Sunday school teacher, and got involved in the praise and worship team. At age thirty-one, I got remarried to Anthony, whom I believed was God-directed, only to discover that he could become extremely domestically violent. Upon that discovery, I filed for a divorce about one year after.

Failure in my second marriage was another major crisis in my life, but God used this to propel me into the missionary call on my life. I resigned from teaching and spent four years in Colombia as a missionary. They were four of the best years in my teaching career, even though I was not receiving a salary. God used me in ways that I never conceived of—in the area of preaching and teaching His Word, deliverance ministry, as a marriage counselor, an interpreter and translator, and a Bible school director.

God taught me how to live by faith, and to trust Him to provide for my every need. God showed me that even though my seven-year marriage ended in divorce because of practicing infidelity and continuous unfaithfulness on my husband's part, the one semester that I experienced at West Indies School of Theology and the pastoral ministry that I was involved in, all served to prepare me and launch me into being an effective missionary and translator/interpreter in Colombia, a committed leader of prayer and Bible study groups in public schools, a founder/director of a Christian television program, a founder/director of a prayer vigil ministry.

My failed marriages served to give me informal training in marriage counseling, and while in Colombia as a missionary, God sent many married couples to me for advice. With God's help, I was able to discern the deep-seated issues involved and I advised them based on the experiences that I endured.

I was introduced to one semester of formal training at the West Indies School of Theology, and this built a genuine foundation in me and a deeper quest for a more profound knowledge and understanding of the Word of God. I studied Homiletics, Hermeneutics, Exegesis, Greek, Hebrew, Praise and Worship, among others. The informal training that I had was "learn as you go and grow." I was being trained by my involvement in my Sunday classes, my youth meetings, my Bible study groups, my church, and most of all, on the mission field in Colombia.

In the spring of 2020, I initiated studies at ORU in the Master's Degree in Christian Ministry. In the fall of that same year, I transferred to the Master of Divinity. I graduated in April 2022 with a Master of Divinity, and I am presently pursuing my Doctorate in Ministry. All these training sessions are being used by God to launch me into the calling that He has for my life.

At ages 33–37, from January 1995 to September 1998, I became a missionary in Colombia, South America and was ordained as a minister. Even though God affirmed my ministry at age eleven and told me that He had called me to be a missionary, there was a need for the timing of that ministry to be confirmed. It is highly possible that the two occasions when I resigned from my teaching job, I might have been outside of God's timing, and because of the hardships involved, I had to revert to the teaching career. However, because I serve a God who works all things for my good, He was able to turn the tables and bring benefits out of my wrong timing and give me the one-semester experience at Bible college as a boost to my future ministry.

At age thirty-eight, in May 1999, I started reading about the life of Mother Teresa while serving as the interim director at the Tucson Prayer House. I was totally impressed by her ministry to the destitute. BJ and Anita, the directors of the Tucson Prayer House, had gone on vacation for two to three months. They had given me the names of the board members so that I could contact them if necessary.

Having read of Mother Teresa's service to the poor, I felt God's irresistible tug on my heart to reach out to the poor and the homeless in the neighboring parks. This godly urge was compounded when a precious elderly couple brought numerous loaves of bread to distribute to a pastor and his congregation, who had started to use the Prayer House temporarily for their worship services. The members turned up their noses and refused to accept the bread. My heart was grieved when I saw their condescending attitude. I went to bed hurting for the demeaning treatment of members of the body of Christ, one towards the other.

That same night, God spoke to me in a vision, "Bread was brought to the church members, and they refused it. Take it to the poor." That was the confirmation I needed from God to inaugurate the ministry officially to the poor and the homeless. God inspired me to call the ministry "This is What Jesus Will Do Ministries," and He instructed me to cook the food for the poor just how I would cook it for myself. I prepared a huge pot of potato and chicken soup, made sandwiches, and called for help and support from the first name of the person on the list of board members that BJ and Anita had left with me. That board member's name was Ernest Baker, and he came willingly, but also cautiously, and out of curiosity to see who this lady with an accent was and why she was seeking help to distribute food to the indigents in the park. He also brought his twenty-eight-year-old daughter Giah with him, and his seven-month-old granddaughter Zaria, as his "bodyguards."

Ernest later told me that he came to help me because his heart had a disposition to help anyone who wanted to do something for Jesus. However, he confessed that he was clandestinely observing me to see the genuineness of what I was doing. He was impressed with my sincerity and authenticity, and the striking and tangible anointing that was evident upon my life.

Ernest faithfully accompanied me to the park every Sunday morning, and I would walk around the parks to where the homeless people were, playing the guitar, singing, and preaching to them. I literally felt "like Jesus" as I did so, and it reminded me of when Jesus looked with compassion upon the multitude of people who were following him. Not only did He heal them from sickness and deliver them from demonic oppression and possession, but he took care of them physically, as was evidenced in the feeding of the multitude of 5,000 people (Luke 9: 10–17).

The name of my ministry, "This Is What Jesus Will Do Ministries," was further substantiated and continued to be birthed out of these ventures. Ernest and I were ordained as ministers by Pastor Grant, whose ministry was affiliated with World Harvest Church. At age thirty-eight, on November 25th, 1999, Ernest and I got married by Pastor Grant at the Tucson Prayer House after six months of courtship. It was Thanksgiving Day and most of our wedding guests were the poor and homeless, who usually were invited to eat at the Prayer House every Thursday. Ernest and I decided to exemplify Luke 14:23: "Then the master said to the servant, 'Go out into the highways and hedges, and compel them to come in, that my house may be filled.'"

The few immediate family members and close friends who

were invited to come to the Prayer House were not told that it was our wedding celebration that they were attending. Words are inexpressible to describe the joyous screams of huge surprise exhibited by Giah, his twenty-eight-year-old daughter, and Dominique, his twenty-six-year-old son when Ernest and I appeared in our wedding apparel. Charity, his ten-year-old granddaughter, was awestruck.

Ernest and I were introduced to Access Tucson television studio by a homeless man. We both underwent training, and in October 1999, I became the director/producer of a Christian television ministry called "This Is What Jesus Will Do Ministries." At age thirty-nine, in January 2000, I started pioneering/pastoring a church alongside my husband in Tucson, Arizona.

On New Year's Eve in 2002, I asked my husband to take me to a church that I had never attended before. At thirty-five weeks pregnant, I was in no mood to cook dinner, and I was hungry. My husband took me to the Door Christian fellowship, and as we entered, they were serving dinner! What a Mighty God we serve! God answered my silent prayer for food, and I was overly grateful and joyful.

At the start of January 2002, I relinquished my pastoral ministry because of the low church growth, and also because

I felt the need for support, as I was eight months pregnant with my first daughter. I relocated into the Door Christian Fellowship Church, along with my husband.

At age fifty-seven, I became the founder /director of a prayer vigil group in Yuma, Arizona. Even though I was married, it was a time of aloneness with God. I had to trust Him for every need in my life and in dealing with my children, moment by moment. I learned to walk by faith and not by sight, and as a result, I developed a deep intimacy with the Lord. God transitioned me from founder/director of the prayer vigil ministry (where I endeavored to bring pastors together to pray on the last Friday of each month for three hours from 9:00 p.m. until 12:00 midnight) into prayer vigil for my own life and that of my husband and four children, so that I could hear from Him concerning the direction that He had for us as a family.

God used this short experience that I had in pastoring, and my ten-year involvement in Christian TV ministry, alongside my new husband and my four young children, ages nine, eight, seven, and four, years, to have me relinquish every form of external ministry and be a missionary to my four children and my husband.

God used the prayer vigil ministry that I originated to unite pastors in Yuma, Arizona for once-a-month prayer. It served to promote me into an established prayer warrior/intercessor when I transitioned from Arizona to Victory Church, Oklahoma.

As a wife, a mother, a missionary to my children, and a public school teacher, there was a need to develop organizational skills to face these four areas of stress and pressure in my life.

I lived by the motto of Martin Luther who once said, "I have so much to do that I shall spend the first three hours in prayer."[1] This ministered to me so much that God even gave me a song based on it:

> Send Your Revival in my soul!
> Send Your Revival in my soul!
> I have got so many things to do,
> So, I am crying out to you,
> Send Your Revival in my soul!

At age fifty-eight, I relocated from Arizona to Oklahoma to be where God wanted me to be—at Victory Christian Church and Oral Roberts University. I started attending ORU to pursue my masters in Christian ministry. The following semester, I transferred to the master of divinity upon the recommendation of one of the professors. During those years, I attended early morning prayer, Monday to Friday, and God used me as a prayer warrior/intercessor.

I taught Spanish at a public school in Tulsa, and I believed God had me there for such a season to bring healing and deliverance to my students. I am presently teaching first graders in the Tulsa Public School District, and the challenges are incredibly great. I firmly believe that God transitioned me from high school to elementary school to show me at what level students' behavioral issues arise, or even before then, and certainly in the home.

I host a connect group for Victory Christian Church in my home for Hispanics and it is called Andando por La Fe y No por La Vista—Walking by Faith and Not by Sight. The connect group is now transformed into a bilingual group. It is extended to whomever wants to attend.

During my ministry Practicum Field Ministry, I did my internship at Iglesia Hispana, Victory, and upon completion, I was asked to teach at their Bible Institute.

During the period from December 7 to February 5, I campaigned as a candidate for the TPS school board. I operated by blind faith and resigned my teaching position so as not to create a conflict of interest. I openly projected Jesus as the only solution for the school issues and resulting from the spiritual boldness that I exhibited in the campaign, pastors and evangelists contacted me to invite me to do conferences at their church. Presently, I am doing an online Bible study every Saturday morning with a Pakistani evangelist and his congregation. A pastor from Sierra Leone contacted me to connect with his network of pastors to do a pastors' conference in November. I will be leaving for Sierra Leone in five weeks.

In the spring of 2022, I went on a mission trip to Belize for one week, and in the summer, I went on another mission trip to Costa Rica for one week. I was invited to go to Sierra Leone in November to host a pastors' conference and do revival services for one week. I told the pastors that I would go only if God authorizes me. While on the mission trip in Belize, God confirmed to me that I should go, and right away He gave me the theme for the conference: "Pastors, Called to Pastor by the PASTOR of Pastors."

My heart's desire is to become fully integrated into full-time ministry, and as soon as God opens the doors, I will enter. My heart is for mass evangelism, and God has given me a vision of myself hopping from one airplane to the next, doing what

He has called me to do, and moving on. There is a sense of urgency to do what He has called me to do. I thought that God was calling me just to the Hispanic world, but He has extended my vision and is enlarging my borders to Africa and Asia.

My desire is to win the lost at any cost, and the vision and mission of ORU resonates with me: "Go where God's light is dim, where God's voice is heard small, where God's healing power is not known, even to the uttermost bounds of the earth."

"FOR A DAY IN YOUR COURTS IS BETTER THAN A THOUSAND. I'D RATHER BE A DOOR KEEPER IN THE HOUSE OF GOD THAN TO DWELL IN THE TENTS OF WICKEDNESS."
(PSALM 84:10)

"FOR I THE LORD YOUR GOD HOLD YOUR RIGHT HAND, IT IS I WHO SAY TO YOU, FEAR NOT, I AM THE ONE WHO HELPS YOU."
(ISAIAH 41:13).

Chapter Five

Junegrid and the

Necessity of Apologetics

I HAVE KNOWN JUNE BAKER FOR TWENTY-FOUR
YEARS. JUNE IS A GODLY WOMAN. SHE HAS BEEN A
MISSIONARY FOR SEVERAL YEARS. TO THIS DAY, SHE
DOES MANY MISSION TRIPS, EVEN THOUGH SHE HAS
GONE THROUGH MANY OBSTACLES IN HER LIFE.
NO MATTER WHAT TRIALS SHE GOES THROUGH, SHE
TRUSTS THE LORD FOR EVERY ASPECT OF HER LIFE.

Sara Holowell

Vice President of Hope for the Harvest

(operates in the prophetic)

***

This book will be incomplete if I fail to adorn this chapter
with my research paper on the "Necessity of Apologetics,"
which I submitted for my apologetics class in the spring
of 2022 to Dr. James Burkett, professor at Oral Roberts
University.

Complying with the suggestion of Denise Thompson (a fellow University of the West Indies, St. Augustine, Trinidad alumni graduate from our 1979–1982 Intervarsity Christian Fellowship Prayer Team) to submit one of my MDiv research papers from ORU for the American Scientific Affiliation (ASA) Convention, I submitted my research paper on "The Necessity of Apologetics," and I was selected to do a poster presentation of this research paper at the ASA Convention at Point Loma Nazarene University in July 2022.

Prior to this class, I ignorantly despised anything that pertained to apologetics, and even the sound of the word itself. I must give credit to my professor Dr. James Burkett for teaching the class with such intense fervor and vibrancy that he made me fall in love with apologetics.

It behooves me to affirm at the very onset of this paper that a Christian's lifestyle that reflects the Beatitudes in Matthew 5: 3–10 and the Fruit of the Spirit in Galatians 5: 22–26 are great non-verbal apologetic tools. Observing the attitude of Leslie, Lee Strobel's wife, in *The Case for Christ*, she inadvertently employed apologetics.[2] The redemptive work of salvation inevitably produced a change in Leslie, and she developed a deep and intimate relationship with Jesus. Lee opposed and challenged his wife's conversion to Christianity. Unknown to his wife, Lee embarked on a quest to disprove Christianity and debunk Jesus. It was interesting and ironic that Lee, even though he was an avowed atheist, because he was an award-winning journalist, used his skill to research and investigate the truth about Jesus.

As said earlier, Leslie, unknowingly, was utilizing apologetic tactics. It is noteworthy that while Lee's life spiraled downhill into anger, bitterness, and alcohol, his wife's life spiraled uphill into a faithful, steadfast, and loving wife amid the challenges of being tried and tested. Leslie was, in fact, providing a defense for her Christian faith. Leslie was able to arrive at this peak in her life through intimacy with God via prayer, Bible study, church attendance, and water baptism. Leslie's spiritual experience and growth resulted from the miraculous and regenerative work of the Holy Spirit in her life because of her complete surrender to God.

The necessity of apologetics is inbuilt or innate in the heart of every Christian—it just has to be uncovered or discovered. Leslie continually exhibited faith in Jesus and focused on her heart and personal experiences. Her favorite verse that she prayed consistently for her husband's conversion was Ezekiel

36:26: "And I will give you a new heart, and a new spirit I will put within you. And I will remove the heart of stone from your flesh and give you a heart of flesh." Leslie also held on to the authority of the Word of God in 1 Corinthians 7:13–14, believing that her opposing husband, who was contemplating divorce, would become a believer in Jesus and that their marriage would be a success: "And a woman who has a husband who does not believe, if he is willing to live with her, let her not divorce him. For the unbelieving husband is sanctified by the wife, and the unbelieving wife is sanctified by the husband; otherwise, your children would be unclean, but now they are holy."

Leslie's meek and quiet spirit indeed was the apologetic strategy that was used to bring about her husband's conversion. At the culmination of Lee's investigation, Lee locked himself in his room and reviewed his research, concluding that the biographies of Jesus (the Gospel) can be trusted. Lee acknowledged his errors by asserting, "All right, God, you win!." He tearfully confessed to his wife that he was torn apart and scared when she became a Christian, and he set out to prove that she and Christianity were wrong. Leslie used the apologetic tool of the Word of God in John 1:12 and explained to Lee about the gift of Salvation. Lee prayed to God and embraced the Christian faith.

Apologetics "deals with giving reasons or evidence to support Christianity, defending the faith, defeating false ideas, destroying speculations raised up against the knowledge of God" (Koukl, 25).[3] In an effort to clarify the definition of *apologetics*, it is necessary to understand that the term *apology* from which *apologetics* is derived, has two meanings. One meaning is "an acknowledgment of an offense," and the other is "a defense for a person's belief" (Chilton, 3).[4] Chilton emphasizes that apologetics deals with the latter meaning, and states vehemently that apologists do not apologize for their faith; apologists defend their faith. Ambiguities regarding the definition of *apologetics* are removed by the way in which Chilton dissects the compound word *apologia*, the Greek translation for *apology*. *Apo* means from, and *logia/logos* means word, reason, or logic. Therefore, *apologia* comes from the word, from reason, and from logic. *Apologetics* really means "the defense of Christian beliefs and of the Christian way against alternatives and criticism (King, foreword).[5]

The definition of *apologetics* is clearly revealed in 1 Peter 3: 14b–16: "But even if you should suffer for what is right, you are blessed. Do not fear their threats; do not be frightened. But in your hearts, revere Christ as Lord. Always be prepared to give an answer to everyone who asks you to give the reason for the hope that you have. But do this with gentleness and respect." As the verse expounds, "the purpose of Christian Apologetics is to rationally examine the beliefs of Christianity in order to give a reason for the hope that is in us" (King, 3).[6]

The latter command to Christians in this verse "but do this with gentleness and respect" is very crucial when considering the definition of *apologetics*. In David Shibley's foreword to Daniel King's *Proof God Is Real,* he states:

> Dr. King writes with warmth, breadth, and courtesy. Rather than the side-stepping objections to faith, he addresses many of the toughest issues with well-informed arguments and candor. Yet he is never combative because arguments never convince others to change their opinions. Every assertion he makes is embedded in his concern for the reader's spiritual wellbeing
>
> King, foreword.[7]

Gregory Koukl states in *Tactics* that Jesus said when we find ourselves as a sheep amid wolves, we have to be innocent but shrewd (Matthew 10:16). Koukl calls this a "more excellent way." "Even though there is real warfare going on, I think our engagements should look more like diplomacy than D-Day" (Koukl, 35).[8] Koukl underscores that Christians have to demonstrate a kind of relaxed diplomacy instead of confrontation when using apologetics. They must be able to "navigate smoothly and gracefully through hazardous encounters" (Koukl, 26).[9]

King's approach epitomizes the definition of *apologetics*. The definition of *apologetics* cannot exclude the desire of the apologist to lead his opponent to Christ. Jim Burkett states in the foreword of *Proof of God is Real,* "Apologetics clears the way for evangelism. Apologetics leads a person to the reasonableness of Christianity and to the place where he can hear the Gospel of Christ and make a choice." (King, foreword).[10]

I am personally convinced that apologetics gives Christians the opportunity to be strengthened and developed in their faith and trust in God, in Christ, and the Bible, as they intentionally defend biblical claims when they are opposed. Christians need to understand that Christianity is not just a mere religion, but that, in addition to it being a faith that operates in supernatural manifestations, it is a faith that is substantiated by scientific, historical, archaeological, and philosophical facts.

It is also impressive to me how the dominating worldview or non-biblical belief system of any culture can be transformed into a Christian worldview as it is shaped and influenced by the impact of the defended gospel. Chilton mentions that the seven major worldviews are atheism, agnosticism, pantheism, panentheism, polytheism, deism, and theism.

Chilton proceeds to explain that atheists do not say they are ignorant about God's existence. They say that they are adamant that God does not exist. Atheists do not believe in the existence of God. Chilton objects and states that atheists are practicing agnostics because one of the requirements for an atheist is for him to always know all things. Agnostics state that they have no knowledge of the existence of God.

Pantheists believe that everything is God—that God is an impersonal force and not a personal being. Buddhists are pantheists. Pantheists believe that God is a personal God, that God is in all, that God is a spirit and the universe is the physical body. Hindus and New Age philosophers are Pantheists.

Polytheists believe in many gods. Deists believe in the

existence of a transcendent God who is not concerned with the affairs of man. Theists believe that God is both transcendent and immanent. God is personal and He was involved in creation.

Apologetics is primordial because as Christians defend their faith by answering questions, presenting objections, negating, and clarifying misrepresentations about God, Christ, and the Bible, they would be pulling down strongholds that operate in non-Christians. Apologetics is used to defend the faith and combat unbelief. Dr. James Burkett, my professor of apologetics underscored with great enthusiasm the need for each Christian believer to be able to provide answers to non-Christians' questions about God, Christ, and the Bible.

I have decisively concluded like Daniel King that "no longer can apologetics be viewed as an elective; it is part of the core curriculum for every twenty-first-century Christian" (King, foreword). The impact of "The Necessity of Apologetics" is so powerful upon me that I have requested for Christian Apologetics to be included as a course for the fall semester at the Hispanic Bible Institute where I teach. David Shibley acknowledged, apologetics is "a potent new tool for sharing one's faith" (King, foreword).

I had very limited knowledge of apologetics because apologetics had a questionable reputation for me. I subconsciously opposed apologetics in favor of a leap of faith, believing that God Himself could lead a person to faith without having people use apologetics to bring others to faith. Or, I would wonder why people could not simply exercise faith to believe in God, and not have to rely on evidence to do so. "Jesus exhorts us to give the reason for our faith and not to make a leap of faith in the dark but rather to take a step of faith in the light—in the light of the evidence He has provided in nature, in our hearts, and in history" (Geisler, 11–12).[11]

Whatever previous knowledge I had of apologetics was gleaned from Ravi Zacharias. I was more interested in his distinctive and appealing voice, his erudite and eloquent defense-delivery of the Christian faith, than the content of what he said. I thought his preaching was too deep, intellectual, and repetitive. In other words, I did not think that apologetics was necessary. As a matter of fact, on some occasions, I ignorantly wondered why I had to apologize for the gospel. I erroneously believed that I had to make an apology to people for my Christian stance.

It was very interesting and ironic that I did a Power-Point presentation on Ravi Zacharias' teachings for an online workshop training for Randall Loescher's Teaching Ministries Class. The title of the workshop was "The Truth and Nothing but the Truth—Trusting God's Truth in a Fake News World." I was in fact unwittingly purporting "The Necessity of Apologetics" in the workshop. My slides consisted of the following themes by Ravi Zacharias:

A. Psalm 19

B. Has Christianity Failed You?

C. Jesus Among Other Gods

D. New Birth or Rebirth

E. Recapture the Wonder

F. The Grand Weaver

G. The End of Reason

H. The Lotus and the Cross

I. Who Made God?

J. Why Jesus?

iii) Questions raised as I researched the topic "the necessity of apologetics."

As a result of my research on the necessity of apologetics, the following questions were raised:

a. Did Jesus or any of His disciples use apologetics?

b. Why don't preachers include apologetics in their messages?

c. Why is *apologetics* a foreign word in the Church, and why has its definition been erroneous for so long?

d. Why is there a need for apologetics to defend God when God does not need defending, since He can defend Himself?

e. Is apologetics really an evangelistic tool?

iv) The relationship between *the necessity of apologetics* and *apologetics*, and the relationship between *the necessity of apologetics* and *my life*.

The topic of *the necessity of apologetics* relates to *apologetics* because without a full understanding of what "apologetics" is and why it is necessary for believers to employ it in their daily Christian walk, apologetics will remain as something estranged from the Christian world. Without being educated on the necessity of apologetics, Christians will not embrace the opportunity to defend their Christian faith by providing answers when criticized for their Christianity. Instead, unfortunately, they might start apologizing for being a Christian.

The necessity of apologetics also relates to *apologetics* because there is a need for Christians to be able to explain to their critics that morality is a failure without God. Chilton argues that if there is no God as the atheists believe, then life is meaningless, and there is no morality. Therefore, atheists are not able to call anything good or evil. Chilton states that atheists do not acknowledge any Higher Authority (the existence of God) to define good from evil. Chilton reaffirms that God is personal and the source of all value for theists. The atheists, because they do not believe in the existence of God, cannot call anything unethical.

The necessity of apologetics is essential because Christians need to affirm that "Life without God is not only dangerous eternally, but it is also dangerous in the here and now. Not only are there intellectual reasons for believing in God, but there are also psychological and emotional reasons for believing in God, as well" (Chilton, 67).[12] Chilton has certainly proved his point that not only does life have no morality without God, but life also has no hope without God.

The topic *the necessity of apologetics"* relates to my life because I personally need to be continually strengthened in my Christian faith so that I would not become a reprobate and enter into the deconstruction Christianity fad. I never want to become prideful, thinking that "I have arrived," when there is so much further for me to go. As Paul says, "Let him who thinks he standeth, take heed lest he falls" (1 Corinthians 10:12). I want to be always ready to give an answer to those who oppose my Christianity, and in doing so, I would be "edifying myself on my most holy faith" (Jude 1:20).

The necessity of apologetics resonates with me, and I have become an advocate for all Christians to use apologetics as an evangelistic tool. "Apologetics is necessary for modern evangelism" (Chilton, 4).[13] "Jesus is the greatest of apologists and His apologetics provides an example for every Christian to follow, especially if he wants to be an effective witness for Christ to an unbelieving world" (Geisler, 13).[14]

I am believing God to use me in signs and wonders; I must always be ready to defend God's miracle working power.

Chilton states that God performs miracles to substantiate the existence of God. He defines a miracle as a divine interaction with creation in a way that is beyond the normal operation of events, and he alludes to the numerous miracles that occurred in the New Testament—miracles of healing, miracles of exorcism, miracles of resurrection, and miracles over nature, and I can also testify to miracles that have occurred in my own life.

Another area in which the necessity of apologetics relates to my life is that I have to be able to answer questions such as, "Can a good and powerful God exist in a world of evil?" "Why does an all-powerful and an all-loving God permit such horrible things to happen in life?" I embrace Chilton's referral to *theodicy,* which is an intellectual discipline that seeks to clarify the hidden aspect of God's goodness despite apparent contradictions of that goodness.

It is very enlightening that Chilton dogmatically emphasizes that God is good and powerful and allows evil to bring about a greater good in the end. Chilton clarifies that, according to John 3:16, man has been given the choice to respond to God's love. Freedom is necessary for a person to experience love. Chilton further explains that, according to 1 John 4:16, God is love, and the rejection of God's love leads to evil. Love must be freely given, and love must be freely received. If this is not the case, it is not love. God, the Lover, has offered His love to His beloved creation, and the beloved creation has been given the opportunity to respond to or reject the love that God so freely gave. God is not merely looking on while innocent people suffer. It resonates with me that God is with the victim just as He was with Lazarus when his sisters Mary and Martha told Jesus about their brother's death, and it seemed as though Jesus was doing nothing but delaying. According to Chilton, "God suffers with those who suffer. He is not watching from a distance" (Chilton, 80).[15]

The necessity of apologetics is evident in relation to another prominent and challenging question that I face regarding hypocrisy in the church. It is important to emphasize that Christianity is true even when the church is bad because not all Christians are genuine in their faith; Christianity continues to be true even when the church is bad because the truth of Christianity does not depend upon the behavior of the followers; Christianity is true when the church is bad because Christians do not escape judgment; Christianity is still true even when the church is bad because the changing culture has deeply influenced the church. Christianity is still true when the church is bad because salvation is based on grace and love and not on our good works (Chilton, 85).[16]

Additionally, opposition arises towards my Christian faith regarding natural disasters in the world. Chilton provides me with the answer by stating that natural disasters cannot be called evil if they are part of God's natural order because God designed the world with certain cycles and patterns. Chilton states that even though hurricanes may bring destruction to a certain area, they may bring rain to another region where the crops need irrigation. Chilton affirms that there is natural evil in the world. This occurs because God created the world with checks and balances ingrained in the systems of the universe. When these are contravened, evil occurs. God cannot be blamed, for example, if homes are built in regions that are susceptible to natural disasters.

I have learned from Chilton to defend Christianity by agreeing that it is a fact that evil exists in the world. I must emphasize that Christianity is true because Christians have a better hope and future in heaven. This is supported by the Word of God in Romans 8:28: "All things work together for those who love God and are called together for His purposes." Revelation chapters 21 and 22 also support the fact that we will experience a new heavenly creation. Chilton declares that the answer to the problem of evil is in the death, burial, and resurrection of Jesus Christ (87).

v) Salient information or insight from the topic "the necessity of apologetics" that impacted or affected me personally.

The information that affected me personally was the fact that apologetics can be incorporated into my messages and that not only did Jesus and His disciples use apologetics in their discourses, but apologetics was used throughout the Bible. It is interesting to note that God employed apologetics when He wanted to reason with the people of Judah regarding their superficial relationship with Him: "Come now and let us reason together. Though your sins are like scarlet, they shall be as white as snow" (Isaiah 1:18). God also exhorts us to test false prophets: "If there arises among you a prophet or a dreamer of dreams...saying, 'Let us go after other gods...,' you shall not listen to the words of that prophet, for the Lord your God is testing you to know whether you love the Lord your God with all your heart and with all your soul" (Deuteronomy 13:1–5). "I will raise up for them a Prophet like you from among their brethren and will put My Words in His mouth, and he shall speak to them all that I command him" (Deuteronomy 18: 14–22).

I am impressed that it is biblical to use reason to encourage myself in my Christian faith, and to persuade others to believe the truth of the Word of God. The Apostle Paul preached an apologetic sermon in Acts 17: 22–34. He was on his second missionary journey and spoke to the people on Mars Hill. When Paul saw that the city of Athens was infiltrated with idols, he reasoned in the synagogue and in the marketplaces with the Jews and the Gentile worshippers. Paul's apologetic approach was to find common ground with the people, and he met them where they were—he started with what they knew— the altar with the inscription: TO THE UNKNOWN GOD (v. 22–23).

It was very striking that Paul moved from the *common ground* apologetic tactic to the apologetic strategy of *argument based on facts* (24–29). Paul finally refers to the historicity of Jesus with an emphasis on Jesus' resurrection, which is the foundation of Christianity (v. 30–31). The apologetics of Paul was used as an evangelistic tool to win some of the people to the Lord, and others were reconsidering what they heard: "And when they heard of the resurrection of the dead, some mocked, while others said that they would hear him again on this matter, and some joined him and believed" (v. 32–34).

The Apostle Paul used apologetics when he "went into the synagogue and spoke boldly for three months, reasoning and persuading concerning the things of the Kingdom of God" (Acts 19:8). In Acts 22:1, Paul also used apologetics when he was arrested and falsely accused of preaching and teaching against their laws. He defended himself by stating his ethnicity and talking about his conversion experience: "Brothers and fathers, listen to the defense that I now make before you." Paul also used apologetics when he talked about providing a defense for his rights as an apostle in the area of self-denial: "My defense to those who examine me is this, do we not have the right to our food and drink?" (1 Corinthians 9:3-4). In Philippians 1:7, Paul thanks the saints at Philippi for their support for him during his time of imprisonment: "It is right for me to think this way about all of you, because you hold me in your heart, for all of you who share in God's grace with me, both in my imprisonment and in the defense and confirmation of the Gospel."

It is obvious that Paul rivets on apologetics to preach the Gospel: "Some proclaim Christ from envy and rivalry, but others from goodwill. These proclaim Christ out of love, know-

ing that I have been put here for the defense of the Gospel"
(Philippians 1: 15–16). Paul also states in 2 Timothy 4:16: "At
my first defense no one came to my support, but all deserted
me. May it not be counted against them! But the Lord stood
by me and gave me strength so that through me, the message
might be fully proclaimed, and all the Gentiles might hear it."

It was very interesting to note that in Paul's teachings
on 2 Corinthians 10: 4–5, Paul indicates that apologetics in-
corporates spiritual warfare: "Since the weapons of our warfare are not of the flesh but are powerful through God for the
demolition of strongholds. We demolish arguments and every
proud thing that is raised up against the knowledge of God,
and we take every thought captive to obey Christ." Paul also
used apologetics as he admonished Timothy to "guard what has
been entrusted to you, avoiding irreverent and empty speech
and contradictions from what is falsely called knowledge. By
professing it, some people have departed from the faith. Grace
be with you all" (1 Timothy 6: 20–21).

I received incredible information to support that Jesus
was the epitome of an apologist. "Jesus was the greatest apologist for Christianity who ever lived. Jesus was continually con-
fronted with the need to defend His claims to be the Messiah,

the Son of God. Everywhere Jesus demonstrates a willingness
to provide evidence to what He taught to every sincere seeker"
(Geisler, 11).[17] He spoke boldly to the Jews in defense of the
truth in John 8:31–32 when He told them: "If you continue in
my Word, you are really my disciples. You will know the truth,
and the truth will set you free."

Jesus continued operating in the apologetic ministry when
John the Baptist sent his disciples to ask Jesus if he was indeed
the Messiah. John the Baptist was in prison and was beginning
to have doubts as to whether he had identified the right person
as the Messiah. John the Baptist felt that if Jesus was indeed
the Messiah, he could have come and gotten him out of prison.
In response to John's question, Jesus healed many people in the
presence of John's disciples and told them to go and report to
John all that they had seen and heard Jesus do. Jesus did not
do those miracles to show off, rather those miracles were used
to defend and support His messianic and divine claims, and
served to remove John the Baptist's question and doubt:

> Go and report to John what you have seen and
> heard: the blind receive their sight, the lame walk,
> those with leprosy are cleansed, the deaf hear, the
> dead are raised, and the poor are told the good news,

and blessed is the one who isn't offended by me.

Luke 7:21–23

Discovering that the Apostle Peter used apologetics in his epistles is also very impactful to me. The verse that is used to support the necessity of apologetics, and has become the "Apologetic Banner" was written by Peter:

> But even if you should suffer for righteousness, you are blessed. Do not fear what they fear or be intimidated, but in your hearts regard Christ the Lord as holy, ready at any time to give a defense to anyone who asks you for a reason for the hope that is in you. Yet do this with gentleness and respect, keeping a clear conscience, so that when you are accused, those who disparage your good conduct in Christ will be put to shame.
>
> 1 Peter 3: 14–16

That verse was quoted at the very onset of this research paper, and it is very important to observe that Peter gives three reasons for the necessity of apologetics. The first is that since Christians say that they have a hope, they must be able to explain what that hope is, why they have that hope, and defend the hope. The second is for Christians to defend that hope in love, displaying gentleness and respect towards their critics. Christians must not engage in obnoxious argumentation to demean and shame their opponents. The third is for Christians to realize that the defense they are providing is not to show how intellectual they are, but to defend Christ, and eventually to lead their opponent to Christ.

Even though I have read Acts chapter two numerous times, and I deemed Peter's speech on the Day of Pentecost to be powerful, eloquent, and convincing, it was very enlightening to learn that his speech was, in fact, apologetic. The Holy Spirit brought conviction, and three thousand people were led to the Lord because Peter's apologetic speech appealed to:

1. The miracles of Jesus as proof that He was from God (1 Peter 2: 22);

2. The fulfilled prophecy that Jesus was the promised Messiah) (25–31);

3. The eyewitnesses' accounts of Jesus' post-resurrection appearances as proof that He was God (v. 32). Peter's apologetic sermon was an evangelistic tool to win souls into

God's Kingdom.

In concluding this research paper on "The Necessity of Apologetics," it is indisputable that apologetics is the core of every Christian believer's life, and it is a very powerful tool, if not the most powerful tool of evangelism. I am encouraged to incorporate apologetics into my sermons, not to prove how intelligent I am or to win arguments, but to convert my opponents to Jesus, to strengthen the faith of those who have become weak, and to offer compelling reasons to those who still have not believed. Since Jesus is the greatest of Apologists, and I am a follower and imitator of Him, I will also seek to be an apologist as He was, so that I can experience a confident Christianity, and be an effective ambassador for Him throughout the world. Even the Great Commission that He gave in Matthew 28:19–20 has an apologetic content: "All authority has been given to me in heaven and on earth. Go therefore and make disciples of all nations…teaching them to observe all things that I have commanded you."

"I WILL INSTRUCT YOU AND TEACH YOU IN THE WAY YOU SHOULD GO. I WILL GUIDE YOU WITH MY EYE."

(PSALM 32:8)

"SEND FORTH YOUR LIGHT AND YOUR TRUTH LET THEM GUIDE ME."

(PSALM 43:3)

CHAPTER SIX

COVID WIDOWS:

THE ERNEST AND JUNEGRID BAKER STORY

JUNEGRID BAKER—THERE'S SO MUCH I CAN SAY ABOUT HER. JUNE, AS I CALL HER—WE GREW UP TOGETHER. ACTUALLY, WE WERE NEIGHBORS; WE WERE LIKE SISTERS. I USED TO SPEND NIGHTS AT HER HOME. HER MOTHER WAS LIKE A MOTHER TO ME. EVEN HER SISTERS AND I WERE VERY CLOSE. JUNEGRID HAD A VERY CLOSE RELATIONSHIP WITH GOD AND HER FAMILY. WHEN JUNE TOOK THE COMMON ENTRANCE EXAM, SHE PASSED FOR ST. AUGUSTINE GIRLS' HIGH SCHOOL, BUT WE STILL KEPT THE FRIENDSHIP GOING. SHE GOT MARRIED AND WAS LIVING IN THE USA, SO WE LOST CONTACT FOR A WHILE, BUT GOD BROUGHT US BACK TOGETHER. WE ARE STILL FRIENDS AND I LOVE HER SO MUCH. SHE DESERVES GREAT SUCCESS IN THIS BOOK.

FAREEDA BAKSH

BELIEVER IN JESUS CHRIST

CHURCH USHER AT CUREPE PENTECOSTAL CHURCH

CHOIR MEMBER (AMONG OTHER THINGS)

***

This chapter consists of an article called "COVID Widows: The Ernest and Junegrid Baker Story." It was written and published by Linda Miller in the Sapulpa Times newspaper on June 1, 2022.[18]

You will encounter numerous aspects of blind faith which will bless and encourage your lives.

"I notice people with hearts to serve others are often drawn together. A mutual desire to reach out with love and practical deeds can create special bonds between the givers. This is true of Ernest and June Baker. It is how they met.

In 1999, June returned from missionary work in Colombia to serve as interim director of a prayer house in Tucson, Arizona, eventually pioneering a food ministry for the homeless and poor in the park. As chief cook, she needed someone to deliver food. She perused the board member list. Ernest Baker's name stood out. She wondered, "Could he come and distribute food in the park?" It was a match. Soon their relationship blossomed beyond serving together. They married six months later on Thanksgiving Day, surrounded by friends they served in the park.

Ernest and June's hearts of compassion led to pastoring "Church on the Street," launching a TV program, and Ernest's work with fatherless young men, through his ministry, Absalom, O, Absalom. They were proud parents of four children. June, also a teacher, homeschooled for ten years, while Ernest taught on an Indian Reservation. Ernest coached basketball, taught Middle School and High School, and loved his students.

"Ernest was sociable—a friend to everyone. He talked to people in Walmart and prayed with them. Stories about his Air Force service in Vietnam often got our family laughing–he was quite a storyteller" says June.

The years 2020 and 2021 brought changes to the family. June pursued her Master of Divinity at Oral Roberts University while Ernest traveled from their home in Arizona visiting frequently until his move to Tulsa in 2021. June says, "He loved our church here and was on fire for Jesus."

In early November of 2021 Ernest complained of persistent head and neck pain. Family members urged him to be checked by his doctor. It took a call from his brother in New York to finally make it happen. The ambulance transported him to a large Tulsa hospital.

June arrived later in the afternoon.

While Ernest tested for COVID-19, June prayed for patients and families and "preached to the people."

Ernest spent ten days in the hospital. June didn't leave his side. She says, "I prayed and encouraged Ernest. I read Psalm 56. We talked about many things."

On the day of Ernest's transition to heaven, each of his seven surviving siblings spoke to him on the phone: prayed for him and spoke words of endearment. June recalls, "Our children were all there and a friend was there to support me. We sang and praised God. It was beautiful. We were all crying. He died on November 26th, a day after our twenty-second wedding anniversary."

Ernest's gravesite military funeral at Fort Gibson was a profound experience showing God's love. As June says "Ernest loved students." God allowed a group of twenty high school students to come to the cemetery to witness his military burial. It was their school project. Ernest would have loved having them there. The officiating minister saw the students, went against the norm, and spent time ministering to the teens. She took advantage of their being there to tell them about Jesus.

Ernest would have said, "'Okay, you're here; you are my audience.' The minister did exactly what Ernest would have done. God has a plan. I could not have put that together. God is perfect in all His ways."

"I comfort myself. Ernest is happy. He wants me to go on when I feel sad," says June.

Ernest spent ten days in the hospital. June didn't leave his side. She says, "I prayed and encouraged Ernest. I read Psalm 56. We talked about many things."

Left to right, the Baker family: Theodora, Theorosa, Junegrid, Theojoshua, Ernest, Theodoxa.

Their family laughs a lot over things Ernest did. Today, June smiles and laughs as she talks about their son's prom. "Mom, does dad have any ties? Does he have any dress shoes?" he asks. A few minutes later their son stands before her wearing his father's size 13 dress shoes.

With God's grace, June completed her Master of Divinity and was selected as graduation speaker to Veterans and their dependents in Christ Chapel. June says God gave her the theme, 'Transparency Sets You Free.' Many people came to her afterward to tell her how much her talk meant to them.

June hoped she and Ernest would travel together doing missionary work. She still sees herself going and is currently scheduled to be in Costa Rica in June, and Sierra Leone in November.

With her own future and others in mind, June encourages women to know their life is not over if something happens to their husband.

Her advice is, "Don't die! Don't go into depression. Instead, go forward and fulfill your God-given purpose."

"I WALK BY FAITH AND NOT BY SIGHT."

(2 CORINTHIANS 5:7)

"WITHOUT FAITH IT IS IMPOSSIBLE TO PLEASE GOD HE WHO COMES TO GOD MUST BELIEVE THAT HE IS AND THAT HE IS A REWARDER OF THOSE WHO EARNESTLY SEEK HIM."

(HEBREWS 11:6)

CHAPTER SEVEN

FROM RETICENCE TO ELOQUENCE

JUNEGRID BAKER EXEMPLIFIES "GREAT FAITH." I CAN SAY THAT HER LIFE SERVES AS A GREAT ENCOURAGEMENT. MS. BAKER IS A PERSON WHO HAS SET HER LIFE POSTURE AS A WORSHIPER OF THE LORD. FROM WHAT I HAVE LEARNED FROM MS. BAKER SINCE COMING TO KNOW HER IN 2020, I BELIEVE MS. BAKER LIVES THE LIFE OF A COMMITTED DISCIPLE. NO DOUBT THIS BOOK WILL GIVE THE READER GREAT INSIGHT INTO "WALKING BY FAITH AND NOT BY SIGHT." IT WILL CHALLENGE BOTH NEW DISCIPLES OF CHRIST AND OLDER DISCIPLES TO EXAMINE THEIR FAITH WALK TO BE AN EXEMPLAR OF A CHRIST FOLLOWER.

KEZIA DANIELS

"FOR WE WALK BY FAITH, AND NOT BY SIGHT" (2 CORINTHIANS 5:7).

JUNEGRID BAKER'S LIFE IS A TESTIMONY OF GOD'S FAITHFULNESS THROUGHOUT THE MANY CHALLENGES SHE HAS FACED AND VICTORIES SHE HAS WON. THERE IS NO DOUBT THAT THIS FAITHFUL WOMAN HAS A HEART FOR SERVICE AND A DETERMINATION TO SEE GOD'S KINGDOM PROGRESS. MAY GOD CONTINUE TO REWARD HER STEADFASTNESS

**

Esther—From "Hadassah" to Esther: From "Hiding" to "Starring."

Junegrid—From a "Shake Head/No" and a "Nod head/ Yes" "to an "Infinity of Words."

Like Esther, all the events that took place in my life from birth to my adolescent life, right through to my adult life, served to move me towards maturity in my life and ministry as a whole. Esther and I truly reflected Romans 8:28: "And we know that all things work together for good to those who love God, to those who are called according to His purposes."

The major thrust of God's development is inward. The real training is in the heart of the person where God is doing some growth testing.[19]

Esther was born an orphan and Mordecai, her cousin, adopted her as his own daughter. When he enrolled her into the pageantry to compete for the Queen's position, he forbade Esther from revealing her Jewish nationality and family background, and her relationship to him. She obeyed and continued to follow her father's instructions, just as she had done when Mordecai was bringing her up. She also relinquished her Hebrew name "Hadassah" for a Persian name, "Esther." During that time of hiding, as the name "Hadassah" implies, Esther was under preparation for the Queen pageantry by engaging in twelve months of beauty treatments of soaking herself in oils of myrrh for six months, and in perfumes and cosmetics for another six months.

Esther's physical preparation of her body is analogous to Esther being in isolation and intimacy with the Holy Spirit, inundating herself in prayer, praise, and worship; and Bible study, developing her inner self.

Meanwhile, Mordecai refused to kneel down and pay homage to Haman. This caused Haman to become enraged, and he decided to destroy Mordecai and all of his Jewish people.

At that point, Mordecai told Esther that she could no longer remain incognito as he had previously requested. She had to go before the king, reveal her Jewish identity and her family background, her relationship to Mordecai, and plead for the deliverance of her Jewish people.

Esther did not want to go. She was intimidated to go before the king because she was self-consumed and feared that she would be put to death for going to the king uninvited. Mordecai reiterated that Esther could not remain silent, because if she did, she and her father's family would perish, and deliverance for the Jews would come from someone else. Esther realized the gravity of the situation, and told Mordecai to assemble all the Jews in Susa in order for them to fast for her, and that she and her maids would fast too. She stated that after the three days of fasting, she would go before the king to advocate and petition for her people, and that if she perished, she perished. I (Junegrid) like Esther, had been transformed from a shy, fearful, introverted, self-centered young lady into a "walking-by-faith-and-not-by-sight," compassionate, self-sacrificing, bold, fearless, strong, assertive leader.

These qualities came only through fasting and prayer. It is exactly what Jesus told His disciples when they could not cast out a demon. "You have little faith. Some things come only by prayer and fasting" (Matthew 17:20). Prayer and fasting brought Esther's flesh under subjection to the Spirit of God, and she was able to demonstrate the fruit of the Spirit, namely patience, love, self-control, peace, meekness, humility, and long suffering.

Esther applied lots of tact and wisdom. She did not lose control and scream at Haman. Neither was she impetuous nor impulsive. She did not blurt out her request immediately and rashly before the king. She was respectful, humble, and waited until the king extended the gold scepter to her. Then she waited again, shrewdly spreading out the situation over a two-to-three-day time period, and invited Haman to come to the banquet with the king. This was well-thought out by Esther. She acted wisely and diplomatically, and gained continuous favor from the king as he kept asking her for more requests. Even then, Esther did not petition for the Jews. She waited for the following day and invited the king and Haman to another banquet.

A life of total surrender and devotion to God was the key in moving Esther into inner strength and maturity, thereby enabling her eventually to fulfill her ministry and calling. "Surely she had come to the Kingdom (her royal position) for such a time as this" (Esther 4:14).

Would Esther have fulfilled her ministry and the call of God in her life if she had disobeyed Mordecai "and refused to come" in the same way that Queen Vashti disobeyed king Ahasuerus and "refused to come"?

"THE STEPS OF A GOOD MAN ARE ORDERED BY THE LORD."

(PSALM 37:23)

Chapter Eight

Sing Out My Soul to the Lord!

THANK YOU, JESUS, FOR MY FRIEND JUNE. MY FRIEND WHOM I'VE PRAYED WITH AND CRIED WITH. MY FRIEND WHOM I'VE "RAISED A FAMILY WITH." WHAT CAN I SAY AND HOW CAN I EXPRESS IT? IT SEEMS I AM LOST FOR WORDS. I PRAY I WILL SPEAK ONLY WHAT YOU SEND TO ME, LORD JESUS.

AS A CHRISTIAN WOMAN, I KNOW IT IS YOU, JESUS, WHO HAVE LED ME THROUGH LIFE AND RECOVERY. YOU TAUGHT ME THAT TRANSPARENCY IS NEEDED TO FOLLOW YOU. TRANSPARENCY BRINGS CLARITY AND FREEDOM. LETTING GO OF THE PAST BRINGS US CLOSER TO YOU, LORD. WE HAVE ONLY TO FOLLOW IN ALL YOUR STEPS. YOU SPEAK THE TRUTH, LORD. YOU LEAD ME TO GREEN PASTURES. YET YOU UNDERSTAND WHEN I DRAG BEHIND, PROCRASTINATE, AND TURN AWAY. I PRAY THAT I ONLY SPEAK IN LOVE TO BUILD UP AND NEVER TO TEAR DOWN.

THANK YOU, LORD, FOR BRINGING JUNE INTO MY LIFE. LORD, THIS IS JUNE'S STORY TO TELL. IT HAS BEEN A PRIVILEGE TO BE WITH JUNE DURING EXTREME CIRCUMSTANCES AND VULNERABILITY. THANK YOU FOR ALWAYS REPLACING OUR FEAR WITH FAITH AND FOR SUSTAINING US. THANK YOU FOR PROVIDING THE STRENGTH THAT WE HAVE NEEDED TO SUSTAIN OUR

LOVE FOR YOU, JESUS. THANK YOU FOR TODAY AND TOMORROW. THANK YOU FOR THE BRIGHT FUTURE THAT IS TO COME AND FOR THE EXPERIENCE WE HAVE YET TO HAVE.

LORD, THIS IS JUNE'S STORY TO TELL. WHY CHOOSE ME, LORD? I KNOW IT WAS YOUR PLAN THAT I SHARE THIS EXPERIENCE OF LIFE WITH MY FRIEND. BUT WHERE DO I BEGIN? HOW DO I EXPLAIN WHAT HAPPENED? WHEN WILL I UNDERSTAND WHY YOU HAVE ALLOWED US TO BE BROKEN AND WHY YOU ALWAYS HEAL?

I DO KNOW THAT WE ARE COMPLETELY DEPENDENT ON YOU, JESUS. I DO KNOW THAT YOU ARE GREATER THAN OUR CIRCUMSTANCES, JESUS. YOUR GRACE HAS KEPT ME POSITIVE, SO I WILL REJOICE IN YOU LORD, NOT IN MY STRENGTH BUT IN YOURS. SO HERE I GO.

DEAR LORD, I HAVE WITNESSED YOUR MIRACLES WITH JUNEGRID BAKER. I HAVE EXPERIENCED JUNE'S CONSTANT PRAYER, FAITH, AND MINISTRY. THROUGH JUNE, I HAVE EXPERIENCED THE MIRACLE OF PREGNANCY AND THE BIRTH OF FOUR CHILDREN. LORD, IT WAS YOU WHO HEALED A WOMB AND PREVENTED THE DEATH OF A CHILD. LORD, THANK YOU FOR PROVIDING SUPERNATURAL PROTECTION IN TIMES OF DOMESTIC VIOLENCE AND FOR RECOVERY FROM MENTAL HEALTH CRISES. LORD, WHEN WE WERE ISOLATED FROM OUR CHILDREN AND ABANDONED BY OUR SPOUSE, YOU NEVER LEFT OUR SIDES. LORD,

YOUR COMPANIONSHIP IS CONSTANT AND EVERLASTING. LORD, YOUR DIRECTIVES ARE ALWAYS CORRECT. LORD, I THANK YOU FOR DELIVERING US FROM INFIDELITIES; FOR PROVIDING SAFETY IN TRAVEL; FOR ALLOWING CITIZENSHIP IN MULTIPLE COUNTRIES. LORD, YOU GAVE WISDOM WHILE HOMESCHOOLING AND GUIDANCE WHEN SINGLE PARENTING. THANK YOU FOR GROWTH THROUGH PUBLIC AND PRIVATE EDUCATION; FOR THE COMFORT OF NEW HOMES IN NEW TOWNS, IN NEW CITIES, IN NEW COUNTIES, AND IN NEW STATES; FOR NEW CHALLENGES, MINISTRIES, ACHIEVEMENTS, AND TRIUMPHS.

LORD, THANK YOU FOR THE REUNIFICATION OF FAMILIES. THANK YOU FOR A BRILLIANT FUTURE FULL OF GOOD WORKS. I PRAY THAT JUNE CONTINUES TO WORSHIP YOU AND PRAISE YOU. MAY OUR TRANSPARENCY SET US FREE FROM OUR PAST REGRETS AND FEARS OF THE UNKNOWN. MAY OUR FUTURE MOVE US CLOSER TO YOU AS WE YIELD OUR CONTROL TO YOU.

NURSE DEBBIE AGRIESTO

YOUR SISTER IN CHRIST

***

For lo, the winter is past,

The rain is over *and* gone.

The flowers appear on the earth;

The time of singing has come,

And the voice of the turtledove

Is heard in our land.

The fig tree puts forth her green figs,

And the vines *with* the tender grapes

Give a *good* smell.

Rise up, my love, my fair one,

And come away!

Solomon 2:11–13

From my childhood days, I would wake up every morning at five o'clock singing.

My mother reported to me that the neighbors would ask her, "Why does your child wake us up every morning at five crying?"

My mother very apologetically said to them, "She is not crying, she is singing!"

Throughout my entire life, up to this day, I have never used an alarm clock. I have an internal clock that wakes me up at five every morning. I have recognized that "clock" to be the Holy Spirit, who wakes me up to come apart with Him. I play the guitar and sing, praise and worship, I pray and intercede for family, friends, and the world, I study and meditate on the Word of God, and I travail and groan and drift back into sweet sleep, wake up at six, get showered and dressed, look my best for Jesus, and leave at 6:30 for morning prayer at church.

The song "You Chose Me" by Paradise Community Church has become my theme song.

Childhood and Adolescent Heartfelt Missions Prep songs:

"ALL TO JESUS I SURRENDER"

BY JUDSON W. VAN DEVENTER

All to Jesus I surrender,

All to Him I freely give;

I will ever love and trust Him,

In His presence daily live.

Refrain:

I surrender all,

I surrender all;

All to Thee, my blessed Savior,

I surrender all.

All to Jesus I surrender,

Humbly at His feet I bow;

Worldly pleasures all forsaken,

Take me, Jesus, take me now.

All to Jesus I surrender,

Make me, Savior, wholly Thine;

Let me feel the Holy Spirit,

Truly know that Thou art mine.

All to Jesus I surrender,

Lord, I give myself to Thee;

Fill me with Thy love and power,

Let Thy blessing fall on me.

All to Jesus I surrender,

Now I feel the sacred flame;

Oh, the joy of full salvation!

Glory, glory, to His Name!

"IS YOUR ALL ON THE ALTAR"

BY ELISHA A. HOFFMAN

You have longed for sweet peace,

And for faith to increase,

And have earnestly, fervently prayed;

But you cannot have rest,

Or be perfectly blest,

Until all on the altar is laid.

Refrain:

Is your all on the altar of sacrifice laid?

Your heart does the Spirit control?

You can only be blest,

And have peace and sweet rest,

As you yield Him your body and soul.

Would you walk with the Lord,

In the light of His word,

And have peace and contentment alway?

You must do His sweet will,

To be free from all ill,

On the altar your all you must lay.

Oh, we never can know

What the Lord will bestow

Of the blessings for which we have prayed,

Till our body and soul

He doth fully control,

And our all on the altar is laid.

Who can tell all the love

He will send from above,

And how happy our hearts will be made;

Of the fellowship sweet

We shall share at His feet,

When our all on the altar is laid.

"SPIRIT OF GOD DESCEND UPON MY HEART"

BY GEORGE CROLY

Spirit of God, descend upon my heart;

Wean it from earth; through all its pulses move.

Stoop to my weakness, mighty as Thou art,

And make me love Thee as I ought to love.

Hast Thou not bid me love Thee, God and King?

All, all Thine own, soul, heart and strength and mind.

I see Thy cross; there teach my heart to cling:

Oh, let me seek Thee, and, oh, let me find!

Teach me to feel that Thou art always nigh;

Teach me the struggles of the soul to bear,

To check the rising doubt, the rebel sigh;

Teach me the patience of unanswered prayer.

Teach me to love Thee as Thine angels love,

One holy passion filling all my frame;

The kindling of the heav'n-descended Dove,

My heart an altar, and Thy love the flame.

"WHERE HE LEADS ME I WILL FOLLOW"

BY ERNEST W. BLANDY

I can hear my Savior calling,

I can hear my Savior calling,

I can hear my Savior calling,

"Take thy cross and follow, follow Me."

Refrain:

Where He leads me I will follow,

Where He leads me I will follow,

Where He leads me I will follow,

I'll go with Him, with Him all the way.

I'll go with Him through the waters,

I'll go with Him through the waters,

I'll go with Him through the waters,

I'll go with Him, with Him all the way.

I'll go with Him through the garden,

I'll go with Him through the garden,

I'll go with Him through the garden,

I'll go with Him, with Him all the way.

I'll go with Him to dark Calv'ry,

I'll go with Him to dark Calv'ry,

I'll go with Him to dark Calv'ry,

I'll go with Him, with Him all the way.

I'll go with Him to the judgment,

I'll go with Him to the judgment,

I'll go with Him to the judgment,

I'll go with Him, with Him all the way.

He will give me grace and glory,

He will give me grace and glory,

He will give me grace and glory,

And go with me, with me all the way.

GREAT IS THY FAITHFULNESS

BY WILLIAM M. RUNYAN / THOMAS O CHISHOLM / ERIC ALLYN SCHROTENBOER

Great is Thy faithfulness, O God my Father

There is no shadow of turning with Thee

Thou changest not, Thy compassions, they fail not

As Thou hast been, Thou forever will be

Great is Thy faithfulness

Great is Thy faithfulness

Morning by morning new mercies I see

All I have needed Thy hand hath provided

Great is Thy faithfulness, Lord, unto me

Summer and winter and springtime and harvest

Sun, moon and stars in their courses above

Join with all nature in manifold witness

To Thy great faithfulness, mercy and love

Great is Thy faithfulness

Great is Thy faithfulness

Morning by morning new mercies I see

All I have needed Thy hand hath provided

Great is Thy faithfulness, Lord, unto me

Pardon for sin and a peace that endureth

Thine own dear presence to cheer and to guide

Strength for today and bright hope for tomorrow

Blessings all mine with 10, 000 beside

Great is Thy faithfulness

Great is Thy faithfulness

Morning by morning new mercies I see

All I have needed Thy hand hath provided

Great is Thy faithfulness

Great is Thy faithfulness

Great is Thy faithfulness, Lord, unto me

HOW GREAT THOU ART

BY REBECCA MALOPE / S. HINE

Oh Lord, my God

When I, in awesome wonder

Consider all the worlds Thy hands have made

I see the stars, I hear the rolling thunder

Thy power throughout the universe displayed

Then sings my soul, my Savior God to Thee

How great Thou art, how great Thou art

Then sings my soul, my Savior God to Thee

How great Thou art, how great Thou art

And when I think that God, His Son not sparing

Sent Him to die, I scarce can take it in

That on the cross, my burden gladly bearing

He bled and died to take away my sin

Then sings my soul, my Savior God to Thee

How great Thou art, how great Thou art

Then sings my soul, my Savior God to Thee

How great Thou art, how great Thou art

When Christ shall come, with shout of acclamation

And take me home, what joy shall fill my heart

Then I shall bow, in humble adoration

And then proclaim, my God, how great Thou art

Then sings my soul, my Savior God to Thee

How great Thou art, how great Thou art

Then sings my soul, my Savior God to Thee

How great Thou art, how great Thou art

How great Thou art, how great Thou art

EACH STEP I TAKE

BY W ELMO MERCER

Each step I take my Saviour goes before me,

And with His loving hand He leads the way,

And with each breath I whisper "I adore Thee;"

Oh, what joy to walk with Him each day.

Each step I take I know that He will guide me;

To higher ground He ever leads me on.

Until some day the last step will be taken.

Each step I take just leads me closer home.

At times I feel my faith begin to waver,

When up ahead I see a chasm wide.

It's then I turn and look up to my Saviour,

I am strong when He is by my side.

I trust in God, no matter come what may,

For life eternal in His hand,

He holds the key that opens up the way,

That will lead me to the promised land.

MY MISSIONARY SONG

(My husband was responsible for encouraging me to record this song, and he personally took me to a studio to do the recording.) He narrated 2 Chronicles 6: 32, 33, 40 at the beginning, middle, and end of the song. As I am penning these words now, I feel very emotional and I could literally hear his baritone masculine voice saying,

Moreover concerning the stranger, which is not of Thy people Israel, but is come from a far country for thy Great Name's Sake, and Thy Mighty Hand, and Thy Stretched Out Arm, if they come and pray in this house; Then hear Thou from heaven, even from Thy Dwelling Place, and do according to all that the stranger calleth to Thee for, that all people of the earth may know Thy name, and fear Thee, as doth Thy People Israel, and may know that this house which I have built is called by Thy Name…Now, my God, let, I beseech thee, Thine eyes be open, and let thine ears be attent unto the prayer that is made in this place.

2 Chronicles 6:32,33,40

I have to stop for a moment to reflect on those precious moments. He always marveled at the fact that he was married to a stranger, a foreigner, a non-American, a Trinidadian, and that God was using a stranger to impact his life and others. Hence his reason for selecting these verses and using them as the prelude, interlude, and postlude for:

"My Missionary Song"

Lord, I want to be a witness

To the ends of the earth

I want the world to know

That you have saved my soul

Lord I'll go and let them know

Your salvation is pure and true

Pain is in their heart

They need a touch from you

Lord, I'll go

To the uttermost ends of the earth

You are with me

To comfort me

Lord, I see the boys and girls, the youth and adults too

Lord since I was a little girl

You placed a desire in my heart

To be a witness for you

To preach Your Gospel true

And now after some twenty years I'm fulfilling Your Perfect

will

As Isaiah said to you,

"Here am I, send thou me!"

Go ye therefore and teach all nations, Go! Go! Go!

Go ye therefore and teach all nations, Go! Go! Go!

Lo! I am with you

If ye love me, truly love me, Feed my sheep!

Lord, I'll go to the uttermost parts of the earth

You are with me to comfort and use me

SOME THROUGH THE WATER

SONGWRITERS: JASON SAETVEIT / RICHARD HALL

In shady, green pastures so rich and so sweet

God leads His dear children along

Where the water's cool flow bathes the weary one's feet

God leads His dear children along

Some through the water, some through the flood

Some through the fire, but all through the blood

And some through great sorrow, but God gives the song

In the night season and all the day long

Sometimes on the mount where the sun shines so bright

God leads His dear children along

Sometimes in the valley, in darkest of night

God leads His dear children along

Though sorrows befall us and satan oppose

God leads His dear children along

Through grace we can conquer, defeat all our foes

God leads His dear children along

Some through the waters, some through the flood

Some through the fire, but all through the blood

Some through great sorrow, but God gives the song

In the night season and all the day long

"O TO BE LIKE THEE"

BY THOMAS O. CHISHOLM

1. Oh! to be like Thee, blessed Redeemer,

This is my constant longing and prayer;

Gladly I'll forfeit all of earth's treasures,

Jesus, Thy perfect likeness to wear.

Refrain:

Oh! to be like Thee, oh! to be like Thee,

Blessed Redeemer, pure as Thou art;

Come in Thy sweetness, come in Thy fullness;

Stamp Thine own image deep on my heart.

2. Oh! to be like Thee, full of compassion,

Loving, forgiving, tender and kind,

Helping the helpless, cheering the fainting,

Seeking the wand'ring sinner to find.

3. Oh! to be like Thee, lowly in spirit,

Holy and harmless, patient and brave;

Meekly enduring cruel reproaches,

Willing to suffer, others to save.

4. Oh! to be like Thee, Lord, I am coming,

Now to receive the' anointing divine;

All that I am and have I am bringing,

Lord, from this moment all shall be Thine.

5. Oh! to be like Thee, while I am pleading,

Pour out Thy Spirit, fill with Thy love,

Make me a temple meet for Thy dwelling,

Fit me for life and Heaven above.

Junegrid Baker's

"My Missionary Song"

"Lord, I want to be a witness

To the ends of the earth,

I want the world to know

That you have saved my soul

Lord, I'll go and let them know

Your Salvation is pure and true

There is no one else but you,

Who can save their dying souls."

"Lord, I'll go

To the uttermost parts of the earth,

You are with me

To comfort me."

"Lord, since I was a little girl,

You placed a desire in my heart,

To be a missionary for you,

To preach Your Gospel True.

And now, after some twenty years,

I'm fulfilling Your Perfect Will,

As Isaiah said to you,

"Here am I! Send thou me!"

"Lord, I'll go

To the uttermost ends of the earth,

You are with me,

To comfort me."

"Go, ye therefore, and teach all nations, Go! Go! Go!

Go, ye therefore, and teach all nations, Go! Go! Go!

Baptizing them in the Name of the Father, The Son, and Holy

Ghost.

Go! Go! Go!"

"If ye love me, truly love, me, Feed my sheep!

If ye love me, truly love, me, Feed my sheep!

Lo, I'll be with you forever and forever

Until the end of the world!

Go! Go! Go!"

"Lord, I'll go to the uttermost parts of the earth

You are with me to comfort and use me!"

"GOD WILL COMPLETE THE WORK THAT HE STARTED

IN ME."

(PHILIPPIANS 1:6)

CHAPTER NINE

<u>SIERRA LEONE, HERE I COME!</u>

I HAVE KNOWN JUNEGRID BAKER FOR OVER TWENTY YEARS. BASED ON HER LIFE HISTORY, SHE PORTRAYS AN EXCELLENT EXAMPLE OF "BLIND FAITH." LEAVING HER NATIVE COUNTRY AND MOVING TO ANOTHER, WHERE THE LANGUAGE AND CULTURE DIFFER FROM HER OWN. TRUSTING GOD AS SHE STEPPED OUT IN FAITH TO DO HIS WORK THROUGH HER. TRUSTING GOD AND GIVING BIRTH TO FOUR SMART AND TALENTED CHILDREN AT AN ADVANCED TIME IN HER LIFE AND USING HER GOD-GIVEN GIFTS AND TALENTS TO RAISE AND EDUCATE THEM TO WHAT THEY HAVE BECOME.

I AM TRULY EXCITED FOR THIS BOOK AND LOOK FORWARD TO READING AND RECOMMENDING IT TO OTHERS.

LENDOR MARKS-BROWN

REGISTERED NURSE, ONCOLOGY CERTIFIED,

CERTIFIED MIDWIFE , PASTOR'S WIFE, CHILDREN'S AND

WOMEN'S MINISTRIES LEADER

TO MY BEAUTIFUL MOTHER:

YOU ARE STRONG AND INTELLIGENT, AND THE BLUEPRINT OF RIGHTEOUSNESS FOR WHICH I LONG

TO BE. YOU HAVE SHOWN ME WHAT IT'S LIKE TO LOVE SOMEONE UNCONDITIONALLY BESIDES OUR HUMAN NATURE. YOU'RE ON MY MIND ALL THE TIME AND YOU KEEP ME ACCOUNTABLE IN WAYS YOU DON'T EVEN KNOW. WITHOUT YOU BEING HERE, I WOULDN'T KNOW THE BASIC STANDARD FOR BEING A GOOD, GODLY WOMAN. YOU HAVE A SOFT HEART FOR PEOPLE IN NEED, WHICH HAS BEEN CARRIED ON TO ME AND FOR WHICH I LOVE YOU DEARLY. YOUR AMBITION IS UNMATCHED BY ANYONE I'VE EVER MET...AND YOU JUST KEEP GOING. YOU DON'T LET THE TROUBLES OF LIFE STOP YOU FROM REACHING YOUR GOALS, AS WELL AS PEOPLE'S HEARTS. YOUR CONFIDENCE, BOTH INSIDE AND OUT, MAKES YOU SEEM INVINCIBLE TO ALL THAT THE WORLD THROWS AT YOU. I THANK GOD EVERY DAY THAT HE BORE ME TO YOU. I LOVE YOU.

THEODOXA BAKER,

JUNEGRID BAKER'S SECOND DAUGHTER

PUBLIC RELATIONS AND ADVERTISING,

ORAL ROBERTS UNIVERSITY

BAKERTHEODOXA@ORU.EDU

***

It took one call from Pastor Kojo. It took one month from me.

I was unsuccessful in my intense campaign as a candidate for the school board, but I was successful as a "candidate" for international pastors who reached out to me to host pastors' conferences for them in their countries. Social media revealed to them the fervor and intensity of my campaigns as I publicly and unashamedly declared Jesus to be the only solution to the major issues that our schools were facing, and this positively impacted the pastors. It must have been God showing these pastors that I had a message to transmit to pastors. One such pastor was Pastor Kojo George of Sierra Leone, West Africa.

My initial response to Pastor George's proposal to host a pastors' conference was, "I don't do anything without the Holy Spirit's leading. I will pray about it and see what God says."

One month after, while I was on a mission trip in Belize, Pastor Kojo called again and as I dozed off to sleep that night in prayer, I experienced such a sweet ethereal peace about going to Sierra Leone to host a pastors' conference, and I had no doubt that it was God's confirmation of the move.

I relayed this joyful information to Pastor Kojo who by

then had started calling me "mommy," and he introduced me to his lovely God-fearing wife and children. Josephine started calling me "mum," and my family rapidly extended so that I became a "grandmother" to more children. Pastor Kojo, my "son" introduced me to Pastor Sessie, the leader of the network of Sierra Leonean pastors, and we started meeting on the third Tuesday of each month from March 2022 to pray for and plan for the pastors' conference in November.

God impressed upon me from the early stages of the planning that I was going to Sierra Leone to bless the people and that He was going to make full provisions for everything that I would need to get me there. I was not going to have to depend upon the host country to provide for me. He was going to be my Source, and God was sending me to Sierra Leone with my sufficiency in Him.

God provided the means for me to purchase the airfare tickets for my son and myself very early in May, and I was able to pay for the very expensive yellow fever shots. The visas and the hotel accommodation were also taken care of. I got donations of packets of rice and beans and sixty pairs of footwear from Pastor Ron Baker's "Bridging Hunger Ministry" for the people of Sierra Leone. I received toothbrushes from

Tulsa Bracers, hand sanitizers from Reverend Linda Miller, fifty prescription glasses from Dr. Dudley, and twenty boxes of assorted protective gear from Aspen Dental. A medical team connection was made between the Drs. Samuel and Kathy Ann Duncan, and Dr. Barbara Hutchinson from the USA and Nurse Nancy Campbell, Nurse Fatima Conteh, and Dr. Jenkins Momoh Pujeh, the eye specialist from Sierra Leone, to take care of the medical needs of the people.

Everything was in place for my departure from Tulsa, Oklahoma to Freetown, Sierra Leone on Saturday, November 19, 2022. There were twelve suitcases of Sierra Leonean "goodies" to be checked in, including two suitcases each for my son and myself with personal belongings.

COVID TEST - DEMONIC HICCUP

I was very careful to research and inquire about COVID requirements on a weekly basis and was informed that there were no restrictions in the USA and in Sierra Leone. However, upon checking in at the reservation desk, much to my amazement and disappointment, I was told it was mandatory for my son and me to produce negative COVID tests results, without which we could not travel. I felt everything inside of me beginning to crumble in fear, but I quickly mustered up enough courage, remembering who I was in Jesus. I looked at the attendant with a smile and I told her that my son and I are leaving for Sierra Leone today because God has mandated it. My prayer language immediately flowed out of my bowels through my lips, and I started engaging in warfare against my enemy, satan, whom I recognized was trying to forestall the supreme blessings that God had for Sierra Leone, through me.

TULSA-DALLAS VICTORY

Thankfully, we had arrived early at the airport, and there were two hours left before we needed to board the plane. We agreed to submit to the state's requirement for the COVID test, called an Uber in which we hurriedly and cautiously loaded the twelve suitcases, found the nearest Walgreens Pharmacy, purchased two COVID home kits, got back to the airport, self-administered our individualized COVID tests, and the results proved to be negative. I was outlandishly elated, and we went to check in our twelve bags and to get our boarding passes.

As we filled out the computerized form for the COVID requirements, the employee finally realized that there was no need for the COVID test. It was exactly as I told them at the beginning that there were no requirements. Satan was indeed trying to inhibit us from leaving. As we were about to get our boarding passes, the attendant said that it was too late because boarding had stopped. Without even thinking, I knelt in the airport, and I said, "God, I thank You that I am more than a conqueror in Jesus' name. Thank You that we would get our boarding passes and get on that plane in Jesus' name. You orchestrated this pastors' conference. You had me meet with the pastors to pray and plan for the conference every third Tuesday of the month for eight months, and this labor was not in vain. You provided all these donations to take for Your precious Sierra Leoneans, and You will not fail me."

I got up from my kneeling position and went and asked to speak to the manager. He responded in a nonchalant manner and told me that I would not be leaving for Sierra Leone today. The next flight would be in three days.

I said boldly, "I am leaving for Sierra Leone today because Jesus said that I am."

He tremblingly checked the computer and gave me two standby tickets to Denver. He told me to go through customs and sit and wait to be called to board the plane. A few minutes after we got there, he appeared and somewhat apologetically switched the two standby tickets for two confirmed seats. He condescendingly said that there was a technical difficulty with the plane, and our flight was being delayed. As a result, we would be able to get on our pre-arranged original scheduled flight as soon as the technical issue was resolved. My son and I got on the plane, glorifying God that He won the battle for us. LONG LIVE INTERCESSORY PRAYER!

I must inform my readers that during this entire spiritual battle, God led me to call upon some forty intercessory prayer warriors whom God assigned to pray for me.

> Finally, my brethren, be strong in the Lord, and in the power of His might. Put on the whole armor of God, that ye may be able to stand against the wiles of the devil. For we wrestle not against flesh and blood, but against principalities, against powers, against the rulers of the darkness of this world, against spiritual wickedness in high places.

> Ephesians 6:10–13

DENVER-CHICAGO VICTORY

You would think that satan, the deceiver, would have gotten the message that his plans to offset my mission were doomed just as he is. However, when I went to retrieve our boarding passes from Denver to Chicago, I was told that I did not have a reservation and that I would have to sit and wait for our names to be called. The employee then quickly told me that there was one cancellation and that I should decide whether my son or I would go on that flight.

Once again, I operated in my identity in Christ. I said politely and emphatically that our flight is reserved, and that we do have confirmed seats. I stated dogmatically with a smile that we are not traveling without the other. I underscored that my son is a minor and we are traveling together. I reiterated that there are two confirmed seats for us, and I thanked the attendant in advance for locating them and for issuing the boarding passes to us. My prayer language started to flow again, and I began doing warfare in the heavenlies, pulling down those strongholds of retardation and opposition. I heard our names announced over the public address system and the flight attendant presented us with two boarding passes for two confirmed seats. Hallelujah!

CHICAGO TO GERMANY – FAVOR AND REST FROM INTENSE SPIRITUAL BATTLES

After a day of spiritual battle, the flight to Brussels, Germany was a welcomed solace and a haven. As I reposed in my seat on the plane, I texted my intercessors that I found a headrest on my son's, Theojoshua's, shoulder. I closed my eyes and reflected on the fact that we are more than conquerors in Jesus' name. I meditated on Isaiah 40:31, which says that "they that wait upon the Lord shall renew their strength; they shall mount up on wings as eagles; they shall run and not grow weary; they shall walk and not faint."

SMOOTH FLIGHT FROM BRUSSELS TO "THE PROMISED MISSION LAND" OF SIERRA LEONE

What a miracle! We were able to get through customs rapidly, and none of our twelve suitcases which contained "goodies" for the "Promised Land" were checked! Pastor Sessie and Pastor George greeted us with a huge embrace and a joyful smile, directed us to a hired taxi, loaded our twelve suitcases, and on the way to the ferry we went to get to Freetown!

While on the ferry that night, I looked at the faces of about one hundred people, and I said to the pastors and to my son that I knew what Jesus would do if He were among those people. I blurted out, "He would evangelize!" As the ferry set sail, Pastor Kojo borrowed my Bible, stood up, and started preaching. Eight minutes into his preaching, two Muslim men ordered him to stop. Pastor Kojo retaliated and said that the Constitution of Sierra Leone allows public preaching. I beckoned to Pastor Kojo to sit down, but he ignored my signal. However, I motioned to Pastor Sessie for him to tell Pastor Kojo to stop because he had accomplished his mission. Pastor Sessie was able to encourage Pastor Kojo to do so.

It was amazing how the incident stirred up the crowd, and the people were summoning for Pastor Kojo to continue preaching. They asked him for his contact number and for the location of his church. One of the Muslim men came and passed right in front of where we were sitting. We lovingly ministered the love of Jesus to him, and he began to be subdued... God's Word never returns void. It accomplishes what it was sent forth to do.

"THE PLANS THAT GOD HAS FOR ME ARE TO DO ME GOOD AND NOT EVIL, TO BRING ME TO THAT EXPECTED END."
(JEREMIAH 29:11)

CHAPTER TEN

LONG LIVE MISSIONS!

IN EVERY SENSE OF THE WORD, MY MOTHER EXUDES BRILLIANCE. AS I GOT TO EXPERIENCE MY MOTHER'S WALK WITH CHRIST FIRSTHAND, I SAW HOW SHE TRULY LIVES BY FAITH AND GOD'S WORD. GROWING UP, IT WAS A GOOD EXAMPLE FOR ME OF HOW A TRUE BELIEVER SHOULD LIVE. I HAVE HEARD MY MOTHER'S MISSIONARY STORY SEVERAL TIMES OVER THE YEARS AND ALL THE HARDSHIPS SHE WENT THROUGH TO BECOME THE WOMAN SHE IS TODAY. I LOVE HER SELFLESSNESS AND JUST THE ALL-ROUND CARE SHE HAS FOR EVERYONE. SHE HAS SO MUCH TO OFFER, AND I'M GLAD SHE FINALLY GETS TO SHARE THIS LITTLE SNIPPET OF IT WITH THE WORLD. I HAVE NO DOUBT THIS BOOK WILL INSPIRE OTHERS AND EN-COURAGE THEM IN THEIR ENDEAVORS.

THEOROSA BAKER

ORU STUDENT

JUNEGRID BAKER'S THIRD DAUGHTER

MY MOTHER IS SUCH A FAITH-LED PERSON. SOME-TIMES I UNDERMINE HOW MUCH SHE WALKS BY FAITH IN GOD, BUT WOW! SHE HAS SUCH A RELATIONSHIP

WITH GOD THAT THE HOLY SPIRIT REVEALS THINGS
TO HER THAT NO ONE ELSE KNOWS, AND EVEN IF
SOMEONE ELSE DID, SHE'D BE THE ONE TO HAVE THE
COURAGE TO SHARE IT BECAUSE SHE HAS FULL CON-
FIDENCE IN CHRIST. THAT'S ONE OF THE MANY THINGS
I LOVE ABOUT MY MOMMA.

THEOJOSHUA BAKER

JUNIOR STUDENT, VICTORY CHRISTIAN SCHOOL

JUNEGRID BAKER'S SON

***

I found it strange and interesting that God had impressed upon me that the Sierra Leonean congregation was going to see me "like Jesus." I refuted, "But, God, I do not want to appear to be God. I do not want it to seem that I am taking Your place." God immediately clarified that the Sierra Leonean pastors and their congregation were going to see me like Jesus in the sense of "servanthood." I was going to serve them, and serve I did in the fullest sense of the word!

I was dumbstruck at the piles of Leon bills that were delivered to me after I exchanged my US currency. I thought that the stack of bills was meant for the bank teller, but when he started telling me how many thousands were in each pile of denominations, the reality of it all struck me. The money was for me! But

God quickly spoke to me in my spirit and said, "No! The money is not for you! The money is for you to sow into the lives of the Sierra Leonean congregation!" I acquiesced because I was now beginning to understand what God meant when He told me in the early months of conference planning that He was going to make all provisions for me, and I was not going there to depend on the people's offering. I was going with a servant-hood spirit towards the pastors and their congregation.

From the very onset of the conference towards the end, God's Spirit of liberality and freewill offering was fully operating in me at the beginning, middle, and end of each sermon. On the second night, Tuesday, God prophetically told me to tell the congregation that they were well poised and positioned to launch out of poverty into prosperity in every aspect of their lives. God told me to allude to Proverbs 13:22: "The wealth of the sinner is laid up for the just." I was able to convince the congregation that they are just because they are justified through the blood of Jesus, and God sees them as just—JUST AS THOUGH THEY HAVE NEVER SINNED.

I also told them that those who have sinned against them by enslaving and exploiting them would have to release their wealth to them as a form of repentance and reparation. I reiterated that they needed to move out of that poised position and venture forth to possess the blessings of prosperity that God had for them. God told me to inform them that all nations shall call them blessed and they will be a delightsome land (Malachi 3:12).

During my message, God told me to bless each member with my widow's mite. Having been a widow for one year, I reached into my huge money bag and gave each person, including children, Sierra Leonean currency of the same denomination. As I walked towards each member, I prayed over them and told them that not only were they being blessed, but I too was being blessed as I, a widow, was giving them what God told me to give them at the moment. I uttered to each one of them, based on the story of the widow's mite in Luke 21:1–4: "God sees you, He commends you, and He defends you!"

My liberality and freewill offering could not cease, and God just had me pouring financial blessings to married couples as I ministered to them and had them renew their marriage vows. They were all called up to sit on the platform, and if their spouse was absent, they were told to sit next to an empty chair which represented the absent spouse. At the end of the marriage vows renewal ceremony, each husband was given a monetary

gift and was told to purchase their wife a love gift to symbolize
and consolidate their love and commitment.

God had me minister unto them about breaking the curse
of poverty on their lives and I referred to Malachi 3:8–12 to
encourage them to start tithing so that God will rebuke the de-
vourer from their lives. I also referred them to Proverbs 3:9 to
show them the importance of first fruits offering.

God led me to give money of a higher denomination to pastors and leaders, and even as I was thinking of giving a greater
amount to them based on their hierarchy, God corrected me and
told me to give to each pastor, leader, and lay person the same
amount to show equality in the body of Christ. I was reminded
of the parable that Jesus told in Matthew 10:1–16 where the
landowner hired men early in the morning and agreed to pay
them the same rate as those who were hired at a later hour.
Those who were hired first grumbled because they thought that
they were going to receive more wages since they had done
a lot more work. The landowner did not listen to their com-
plaints, but asked, "Am I not allowed to do what I choose with
what belongs to me? Or are you envious because I am gener-
ous?" The landowner went on to say, "The last will be first and
the first will be last." As I finished my sermon and the money

distribution, I challenged the congregation to tithe and give freewill offerings from that money that they had just received.

There were occasions when I had to demonstrate "walking by faith, not by sight' to the host pastors. I had to exhibit audacious, tenacious, and vociferous faith. One such time was when the host pastors were concerned that they would have to cancel having the eye doctors visit on the Saturday that was designated for medical care because he was requesting an exorbitant fee. I told them that they should not cancel the eye care event because I believed they could get the money to pay for at least half of the cost. The eye doctor came and did a fabulous job of eye testing and assigning to various individuals the prescription glasses that I had brought with me from Tulsa.

The time came for the payment to be made to the eye doctor and the host pastors became fearful about not having the money. The eye doctor's heart was touched with compassion by what he witnessed that morning as I was giving so generously to the people, and he was inspired to give generously to them, too. He graciously lowered his fee to an amount and God witnessed to me in my spirit that I should take care of those expenses.

Another occurrence was during the feeding of the children.

The host pastors came to me and said the rice and beans would only be enough to feed the children, and the adults would have to sit apart from their children so that the children could eat alone.

I immediately put on my authoritative cap and said, "Everyone will be fed! No one will be turned away!" I immediately thought of how Jesus fed the multitude of 5,000 with five loaves and two fish. I believe Jesus when He said that the same miracles that He did, I could do, and greater! All the children were fed, and the adults took home a packet of rice and beans, which allowed six servings. They were also given footwear, hand sanitizers, toothbrushes, toothpaste, and monetary gifts. On that same evening, the children and their parents stayed back for the birthday celebration of an eight-year-old boy, and they were all served cake and ice cream.

Soon after the feeding program for the children and the medical fare on Saturday, Pastor Sessie, Pastor George, Pastor Campbell, my son, and I went to visit the campus for the Bible School that Pastor Bona constructed. Two days prior to this, Pastor Sessie took me, along with Pastor George and my son, to Pastor Bona's house and he shared the vision that he has to reach primarily the Muslim community where the Bible

Institute is located. He was excited for me to see the Bible

Institute. Right there on the spot, God tugged at my heart to

make a monetary investment into Pastor Bona's Bible Institute

ministry to the Muslims, and I obeyed.

When we got to the campus of the Bible Institute and the

location of the residences, I interviewed Pastor Bona, and he

expressed that he wanted to affiliate with Victory Church and

use the VBI curriculum that I presented to him. He has ac-

commodation for missionaries/professors to come to teach and

prepare students. The following is a faith question that I posed

to Pastor Bona: "Are you willing to start enrolling students

now or are you waiting for the completion of the Institute?" He

replied somewhat in the affirmative, stating that he would like

to have everything conducive for teachers and students like-

wise, before starting.

As Theojoshua and I got back to the hotel to pack in prepa-

ration for our flight back to Tulsa the next day, my son realized

that his iPad was missing. We contacted the pastors to see if it

was forgotten in church, but it was not found. My son quietly

said, "God knows why that happened," and he drifted off into a

deep sleep.

As I looked at Theojoshua on the bed, he reminded me of

Jesus, who was able to sleep on the boat even though the storm was raging outside, and his disciples were fearful. I decided to take a break from packing the suitcases, sat on my bed, and voiced this prayer, "God, please help me to find Theojoshua's iPad. Please show me where it is." As I lifted my Bilingual Bible that was on the bed in front of me, there was his iPad, snugly hid under my Bible. I blurted out loudly into praise and thanksgiving to God in my hotel room. I woke up my son, telling him the good news and trying to have him join me in praises too. He simply said, "Praise God! Hallelujah!" and went straight back to sleep. When he woke up in the morning, he was not aware that his iPad was found, and he enquired about it. When I told him that I prayed and God showed me where it was, he said that he knew it would be safe, and that is why he was able to do like Jesus and sleep during the "storm." What a childlike faith! How impressive!

On Saturday, when Pastor Sessie came to take us to Pastor Bona's Bible Institute, he boldly said to me that I would be preaching in his church on Sunday morning before taking the ferry to go to the airport. I accepted the mandate and quietly prayed and asked God to give me the Word for his church.

At 3:00 a.m. on Sunday, God woke me up and told me that I

should challenge Pastor Sessie's congregation to walk by faith and not by sight, according to 2 Corinthians 5:7. The congregation needed to be reminded that "walking by faith, not by sight" means that even though they may not see God working right now, they should trust and believe that God is preparing them for blessings and relief from what they are facing.

I alluded to the Merriam-Webster Dictionary, which defines faith as "Belief in, loyalty to, and complete trust in God, and as a firm belief in something for which there is no proof." This definition is endorsed strongly by Hebrews 11:1: "Faith is the substance of things hoped for, the evidence of things not seen." I exhorted them to keep moving even though they don't know where they are going, and I underscored this statement with a quote from Martin Luther King Jr.: "Faith is taking the first step, even when you don't see the whole staircase."[20]

I had three points for my sermon, and they were all repetitive. Point 1: Walk and live by faith. Point 2: Walk and live by faith. Point 3: Walk and live by faith. I reiterated that God really wanted them to walk and live by faith. I told them that they all have faith, as Paul says in Romans 12:3: "God had dealt to every man the measure of faith."

According to Ephesians 2:8: "For by Grace you have been saved through faith, and that not of yourselves; it is the gift of God; not of works, lest any man should boast." I explained to them that they exercised faith to repent of their sins, to ask Jesus to come into their heart, cleanse them with His blood, and to fill them with His Holy Spirit. I highlighted Romans 1:17: "For therein is the righteousness of God revealed from faith to faith." I emphasized Galatians 3:11: "But that no man is justified by the law in the sight of God, it is evident, for the just shall live by faith." I underscored Hebrews 10:38: "Now the just shall live by faith; but if any man draws back, my soul shall have no pleasure in him." I discouraged them from drawing back from living by faith.

I explained that we are not only saved through faith, but we should continue to live by faith because we are called to live a faith-filled life. "Without faith it is impossible to please God because anyone who comes to Him must believe that He exists and that he rewards those who earnestly seek him" (Hebrews 11:16).

PASTOR HOWARD SESSIE'S GRATITUDE AND

SENTIMENTS, AND DR. SAMUEL DUNCAN'S REPLY

On the ferry to the airport, God instructed me to sow the numerous remaining stacks of Leon currency to Pastor Sessie's, Pastor George's, and Pastor Campbell's mission ministry. The pastors were overly thankful and elated.

Good day Pastor Junegrid Baker,

On behalf of the pastors in Sierra Leone and community people, we want to extend our heartfelt gratitude and thanks to you and Theojoshua Baker for the wonderful love you showed to us in Sierra Leone.

You spent your time, energy, money etc. to reach and bless our people in Sierra Leone. May the good Lord continue to bless and expand your coast in Jesus' name. May you live long to enjoy your labor in the Lord. May your children honor, obey and serve God to the fullest of their ability in Jesus' name. God will visit them and change their stories in Jesus' name. You will remain to be at the top always, in Jesus' name. The Lord will surely do you good and continually.

We appreciate you all,

Pastor Howard Sessie

Please read this to your children. ↓

Good day to the children of pastor Junegrid Baker,

On behalf of the pastors and community people in Sierra Leone, we are saying a big thanks to all of you for releasing your beloved mother and brother to reach and bless us in Sierra Leone, both spiritually and physically.

We appreciate your love you have for our people in Sierra Leone. God will continue to bless you people in Jesus' Name.

Pastor Howard Sessie

Sierra Leone Team Leader

Good day Doctor Samuel,

On behalf of the pastors, church leaders, church workers, youths from different churches and ministries, children from different churches and ministries, community elders, community youths and children. We want to extend our heartfelt gratitude and thanks to you, your family, and your organization for the medical gifts you sent through pastor Junegrid Baker and minister Theojoshua Baker to help and support us in Sierra Leone medically and spiritually.

We received the gifts from them, and the medical administration went on successfully to the glory of God. People with eye problems were also examined, treated and lenses were given out to them.

You allowed yourself and your team to be used by God to be a blessing to hundreds of people in Sierra Leone. God will replenish you and continue to bless you all in Jesus' name. We love you all.

Thanks,

Apostle Tamba Howard Job Sessie

Sierra Leone Team Leader

Greetings to you, Pastor Sessie, Pastor Kojo, church workers, and the community blessed by the conference in Sierra Leone last week.

I humbly accept your thanks on behalf of the UWI-IVCF Ambassadors group and assure you we are as thankful for you asking and providing us the opportunity to serve the Church of Jesus Christ and associated communities in Sierra Leone. We look forward to hearing the reports from Rev. Baker of her experience with you in SL and exploring more opportunities to serve each other in Christ in the future. Of course, our support for this venture is not yet complete as medications for distribution post-screening via the clinics and doctors are in transit to Freetown after delaying due to the Thanksgiving holiday here in the US.

Written by Dr. Samuel Duncan

Junegrid's Note to the Readers:

BLIND FAITH DOES NOT HAVE A CONCLUSION BECAUSE

MY LIFE EXPERIENCES CONTINUE TO OCCUR, AND I

WILL INCLUDE THEM IN SUBSEQUENT VOLUMES OF

BLIND FAITH.

THANK YOU.

"I PRESS TOWARDS THE MARK FOR THE PRIZE OF

THE HIGH CALLING OF GOD IN CHRIST JESUS."

(PHILIPPIANS 3:1)

About the Author

Junegrid Baker has been an international and bilingual educator for forty years. She has a Bachelor of Arts degree in Languages and Literature, a Bachelor's degree in Education, a Master's Degree in Divinity and is currently pursuing her Doctorate in Christian Ministry.

Junegrid Baker migrated from her native homeland of Trinidad and Tobago in 1995, and went to Colombia, South Africa as a missionary for four years. Junegrid was invited to the United States in 1998 and started a ministry to the poor and the homeless in Tucson, Arizona from 1999 to 2001.

Junegrid was the producer/director of a bilingual Christian television program called "This Is What Jesus Will Do Ministries" at Access Tucson Television Network from 1999 to 2009.

Junegrid is a member of Victory Christian Church, Tulsa, Oklahoma since 2019, and leads a home bilingual connect group called "Walking by Faith, and Not by Sight/Andando Por La Fe, Y No Por la Vista."

Junegrid Baker is an ordained minister and hosted a pastors' conference in Sierra Leone, West Africa, in November 2022.

Junegrid exudes brilliance. She is strong and intelligent and the blueprint of righteousness. She has a soft heart for people in need. She epitomizes selflessness. She does not let the troubles of life stop her from reaching her goals, as well as people's hearts. Her confidence, both inside and out, makes her invincible to all what the world throws at her.

Junegrid truly lives by faith and God's Word. She is a faith-led person. She has such an intimate relationship with God, that the Holy Spirit reveals things to her that no one else knows, and even if someone else did, she'd be the one to have the courage to share it because she has full confidence in Christ.

Junegrid walks by faith and not by sight, because without faith it is impossible for her to please God.

ENDNOTES

CHAPTER FOUR

[1] Luther, Martin, quoted in *Cyclopedia of Religious Anecdotes*, by James Gilchrist Lawson Grand Rapids, MI: Fleming H. Revell Company, 1923, 303.

CHAPTER FIVE

[2] Strobel, Lee. *The Case for Christ.* Grand Rapids, Michigan: Zondervan Publishing House, 1998.

[3] Koukl, Gregory. Tactics: A Game Plan for Discussing Your Christian Convictions. Grand Rapids, Michigan: Zondervan Publishing House, 2109.

[4] Chilton, Brian G. The Layman's Manual on Christian Apologetics: Bridging the Essentials of Apologetics from the Ivory Tower to the Everyday Christian. Eugene, Oregon: Wipf and Stock Publishers, 2019.

[5] King, Daniel. *Proof God is Real.* Tulsa: King's Ministries International, 2020.

[6] Ibid, 3.

[7] Shibley, David. foreword to *Proof God is Real,* by Daniel King (King's Ministries International, Tulsa Oklahoma).

[8] Koukl, *Tactics*, 35.

[9] Ibid, 26.

10 Burkett, James. The Battle for the Bible: Word of Man or
    Word of God /Apologetics Produces A Confident
    Christianity.

11 Giesler, Norman L. Apologetics of Jesus: A Caring Approach
    to Dealing with Doubters., 2009, Baker Publishing
    Group, Grand Rapids, Michigan: Baker Books, 2009.

12 Chilton, The Layman's Manuel, 67.

13 Ibid, 4.

14 Geisler, Apologetics of Jesus, 13.

15 Ibid, 80.

16 Ibid, 85.

17 Geisler, Apologetics of Jesus, 11.

CHAPTER SIX

18 Miller, Linda. "COVID Widows: The Ernest and Junegrid
    Baker Story" *Sapulpa Times Newspaper.* June 1, 2022.
    https://sapulpaherald.com/covid-widows-the-ernest-
    and-junegrid-baker-story/.

CHAPTER SEVEN

19 Clinton, Robert. *The Making of a Leader: Recognizing the
    Lessons and Stages of Leadership Development.*
    Colorado Springs, Colorado: NavPress, 2012.

CHAPTER TEN

20 King, Martin Luther Jr. Twitter Post. January 21,
    2019. 6:15 AM. https://twitter.com/intouchmin/sta
    tus/1087322675498926080.

CPSIA information can be obtained
at www.ICGtesting.com
Printed in the USA
JSHW010714230623
43529JS00003B/16

9 798887 386836